The Apparition

The
Apparition

A Mother-Daughter Reckoning
with Madness and a Brief Study
on Hearing Voices

Tricia Stafford with
Annie Stafford

atmosphere press

For Ron Coleman

A Note on the Use of Language

I use the term "mental illness" with intention in this book. As we explored clinical diagnoses and treatments in the initial stages of our journey, it offered guidance and knowledge. Later, as we engaged with the Hearing Voices Movement, we outgrew the confines of conventional psychiatry, and the label felt like an albatross around our necks. Its connotations were too permanent and pessimistic, leading to unfair discrimination. The terminology also felt outdated and unenlightened, contributing to the stigma, misunderstanding, and widespread fear in our society. It still feels harsh and uncompromising, but we have been almost afraid to utter the term. We preferred words like "challenges," "distress," and the "diversity of human experience." But Annie is no longer opposed to the usage. It feels more accurate to *her* experience. Mental illness conveys the gravity of her situation and the intensity of her suffering. For me, though, the words "mental illness" will never begin to define the wonderful totality of who she is or negate her limitless capacity for growth.

"In the deepest heart of all of us there is a corner in which
the ultimate mystery of things works sadly [...] Without
further explanation or apology, then, I ask you to join me in
turning an attention, commonly too unwilling, to the pro-
founder bass-note of life."

"Is Life Worth Living?"   *William James*

MOTHER

Preface

Most lives are a chiaroscuro of light and dark, and it is with ambivalence that I accentuate the negative here. This will probably not be the worst story of mental illness you will ever read. There are many caring families whose loved ones suffer under strains more burdensome than my own. At times, the lineaments of my narrative might even lean toward the prosaic, as far as these things go. There are no government conspiracy ramblings, no messianic babblings to family and strangers, no sudden decampments in the dead of night or extended flights of psychosis, but there are other departures from the benchmarks of sanity. This is, instead, a rather hushed tale of a mother and daughter's private agonies. In fact, I never imagined a day I would speak of these things, never wanted to burden my children with memories of their mother's terrible anguish or flaunt the severity of my daughter's own trials, but today I elect a different course. I want to testify to the worthiness of those of us who have grappled with extreme psychological distress, for most of us are just like you, the mental disturbance often only a matter of degree. We are usually going through something important and life-changing, trying to deal with and integrate new and old wounds, endeavoring to make meaning of a stunted or disrupted life, and yearning to tell some empathetic soul the curious way our lives unfolded.

DAUGHTER

Preface

Long before my mother's fingers ever struck computer keys to write this book, the contents were etched across the walls of her mind, waiting to be transcribed. Where spoken words have sometimes failed her, writing has always been her cherished medium of expression. However, writing a memoir takes bravery and the courage to repeatedly hold a mirror to oneself and face painful truths. I am proud not only of my mother's dedication to this book but of her commitment to sharing her story to possibly help others. I hope to one day have the courage to complete a personal account of my own as gracefully as she did.

The portions of this book that discuss my journey are shared with my full permission. I believe my mother deserves ownership of her perspective regarding our experiences. I am confident that she has accurately recounted history, and I have allowed her to include excerpts of some of my own writing. I will always value the healing conversations that transpired during this process. Exchanges that usually cracked open the windows of our souls just a little wider.

The details shared in this book were revealed with a higher

purpose in mind. From our suffering, we hope to educate people about the crucial need for better treatment of mental illness and to emphasize the power of love and kindness during times of struggle. We know that our family's story is only one among millions around the world, but we still feel called to share. Because for every person or family who speaks up, we get a little bit stronger, as individuals, as a society, and as a worldwide community.

The largest factor in my "recovery" has been my mother's steadfast love. My father's too, but I believe it was my mother's love that saved me physically. When I felt half in the grave, barely able to tell if my heart was still beating, completely hopeless, my mother stood by me, rock-solid, heart pumping twice as hard to compensate for my own. Although no conventional treatment worked for me, my mother's love always did. During my most shameful moments, when I was sure I had surpassed the limits of her love, screaming that I hated her when it was really me I hated, she still believed I was innately good. To have a mother like mine is a privilege not many are afforded and something I will never again take for granted.

The very personal experiences shared on these pages have allowed me to get to know my mother on a deeper level and given me a better appreciation for what we have been through together. I would like to thank her for bringing meaning to many difficult years of pain. I will cherish this book and its collection of her poignant moments for the rest of my life.

Introduction

When my daughter Annie Laurie was born in October of 1996, the world appeared fresh and golden. Our family had relocated, two years prior, from Long Island, New York, to our present home in Montgomery County, Pennsylvania, following some heavy financial losses sustained during the recession of 1991. At that time, my husband Mike had lost his well-paying job at a Manhattan advertising agency. Our first house was sold at auction after a lengthy foreclosure proceeding, and we were eventually forced to file for bankruptcy. The job search had been long and difficult, and the move away from New York was not easy for me, but Mike now had a promising new job, and we were grateful for this second chance at a full and prosperous life. By 1996, we were back on our feet, ensconced in a quaint century-old house, with rustic furniture in the living room, a cranberry-colored van in the driveway, and this new baby on the way.

My son Joe had just started second grade at the local public elementary school and was still warming to the idea of a new sibling when Annie finally arrived. The morning of her birth was pleasingly crisp and the sky a cloudless, magnetic azure. The name "Annie Laurie" was a sentimental tribute to my mother, who recently died and loved the movie *A Tree Grows in Brooklyn*. She had a soft spot for Johnny Nolan, the charming but troubled father in the story, who poignantly croons the old Scottish ballad "Annie Laurie" while beset by a bout of melancholy. After his untimely death from alcoholism, his long-suffering wife names their newborn daughter Annie Laurie, evoking his kindhearted goodness and a wistful sense of hope.

For the most part, I was a stay-at-home mom during those early years of parenting. I kept a toehold in the outside world by transcribing medical reports at the nearby community hospital on weekends. After many years of long commutes to office jobs in Manhattan, which I hardly cared about, raising young children was deeply gratifying and liberating. There was both a practical and a sublime sense of purpose to my days that I thrived on. It was thrilling to watch my children grow, and I often mourned the passing days, wishing we could slow it all down so I could savor the enchantment and ephemera of their youth indefinitely.

When Annie was seven months old, I started a journal to memorialize this remarkable chapter in our lives. An early entry:

> *Your father and I can hardly get used to seeing your shining face each day. I keep asking myself, "How did this come to be? How did we get so lucky to have this little girl in our lives?" I adore you and cherish you, and I know that this particular bliss of infancy will soon pass and is already fading, as each day inexorably gives way to the next.*
>
> *You made a decidedly gentle entry into the world— your first cry in the delivery room was low-key, with a soft timbre. As a newborn, you were not especially demanding. You cast off your two night-time feedings in good order, and by the end of the second month, we could*

gratefully count on a decent night's sleep.

Within the family fold, you appear quite happy. "Stranger anxiety" has begun to rear its wary head, though, and you are loath to be more than an arm's length from mama or dada. Your brother exists for you in another, more intensely pleasurable realm, and your excitement is barely contained when he blusters through the front door after school or pays you an extra moment's attention. For him, your squeals of delight and baby laughter reach an inspired pitch. And, happily, he seems equally enamored, appreciating you with both enthusiasm and big-brother affection.

* * * * * *

Indeed, Joe could be a touchingly thoughtful son, suddenly appearing in the kitchen with a freshly picked bouquet of flowers for me from our backyard. He was funny, even as a toddler, pretending to fall off the changing table as he slowly dropped, face down, into my arms. Unusually articulate from the start, he experimented with an adventurous vocabulary and amused us with playful lines he repeated from movies. His childhood phases were intense and long-lasting—fireman, policeman, Superman, Batman, FBI agent, airplane pilot; he loved the uniforms, the paraphernalia, the formalities. A neighbor of ours once salvaged an ancient-looking, weather-beaten fire helmet from a musty corner of his firehouse and gave it to him as a gift. It was too large for Joe, but he proudly held that heavy helmet on his head for a good two years, at home, in bed, on the playground, in stores, in restaurants, every place we went. During his policeman phase, my brother, a former cop, bequeathed him his official police hat, handcuffs, holster, and citation book, all of which kept Joe engrossed for another two years. As he got older, his little-boy sweetness and rascally good humor deepened into a subtle wit and intelligent reserve. His interests were equally consuming—WWII history and aircraft, the sinking of the Titanic, and sports, especially baseball. Mike and I alternated reading to him every night, first the carefree fluff of childhood and, later, mysteries, biographies, *Tom Sawyer,* and other classics of young-boy literature. He came of age with *Harry Potter* and devoured each book in the series countless times. He was a "man of few words," but we could usually figure out what made him happy and took great pleasure in his boyhood passions.

It was a tougher thing to figure out what made Annie's heart leap. While her enthusiasm for bedtime reading was unquenchable, her interests were less enduring than Joe's. She could also be prickly, moody, "a character" in her jaunty red beret and colorful costumes. She had a creative and comical flair, spouting delightfully improvised songs as we drove in the car, composing snippets of stories as soon as she could write, always sketching pictures, designs, and fashion ideas, yet her contentment and absorption were usually short-lived.

At times, she was precociously independent and daring. At seven months, she crawled in an impatient, one-legged crab style before shaking it off to walk upright at nine months. When she was barely more than a year old, I left her playing in the backyard one day while I fetched the stroller from the front porch to go for a walk. The catch-lock was fastened on the gate, but a moment or two later, out of the corner of my eye, I spied a tiny figure toddling up the block. It took me a few seconds to realize it was Annie, and as I hightailed it after her, shouting for her to stop, I was slightly aghast at her cleverness and temerity. She had figured out how to unlock the gate in a flash and then wended her way around the house, down the path, and out into the street without the slightest check back at mom. When she was three years old, we discovered her one morning on the front lawn, pajama-clad, hose stretched from the side of the house to the curb, sponging down our van with a bucket of soapy water. We stared at her through the screen door in disbelief, and when she noticed us watching her, she rushed up the porch steps, hose in hand, to tell us the car wash was her "homemade" anniversary gift to us.

Her best friends were a pair of sisters who lived next door, and the sound of those three girls chasing back and forth through our adjoining yards, their animated shrieks and laughter lilting through my kitchen window, was the sound of happiness to me. The sisters, however, only spent half the time with their father; the rest of the time, they were with their mother, who lived almost an hour's drive away. I was close to the sisters and missed them when they were gone, but when they returned each week, the trio's cheerful energy always restored me.

Looking after Annie by herself was often exhausting; she had virtually no patience or tolerance for frustration and could be unremittingly contrary and irritable. Mike once bought her a set of miniature toy blocks painted with the letters "H-A-P-P-Y" and placed them on her dresser as a talisman. I was often desperate for a couple of hours to myself, and one day took her for a tour of a potential nursery school. When the tour wrapped up, and it was time to leave, I gave her a couple of "five-minute warnings," but she cried and carried on as she usually did when it was time to "transition" from one activity to another. I finally wrestled her into her car seat, and as she sat behind me, still ranting, she managed to untie her tiny red Converse sneaker, take a perfect aim, and fire it directly in my face as I was driving. This later made for an uproarious anecdote, but at the time, I was so enraged I had to pull over to the side of the road to cool down and catch my breath.

On another occasion, while spending time with my brother's family in Washington, DC, most of our group toured the Air and Space Museum, something sure to keep Joe engaged, while I attempted to keep Annie occupied outdoors. When both families reconvened on the museum steps, she displayed her keen displeasure at the goings-on by squatting and banging her forehead several times on the cement pavement before I could scoop her up out of harm's way.

I increasingly realized she was a force to be reckoned with and began canvassing the parenting literature—*The Strong-Willed Child, The Spirited Child, The Explosive Child, The Difficult Child, Is This a Phase?*—not only for tips on how to handle her but for reassurance that though her behavior was challenging, it was still in the "normal" range of what parents of children that age could expect.

Despite these turbulent undercurrents, Annie brimmed with warm emotion. She loved to cuddle and be held, resting on my hip with her arms looped around my neck, and she was profuse in her expressions of affection. She had pert Shirley Temple-like features, with a tousle of honey-colored curls, and her sheer physical presence and diverting manner could coax a smile from almost anyone. She was eager to share her perceptions of the world, had a heart for the underdog, and hated to see anyone get picked on. One afternoon when she was in pre-kindergarten, we met a friend of hers from school for lunch. As the children played in the overhead jungle gym, I overheard her friend make several rude remarks to another girl, after which Annie tried to comfort the girl by reassuring her, "She didn't mean that!"

* * * * * *

The summer before Joe started first grade in Pennsylvania, we considered placing him in the local Catholic school; however, when we visited this new school, we were put off by its dark hallways and dreary atmosphere. We opted instead for the "blue-ribbon" public school system, our branch on the site of a famous Revolutionary War battle. When it came time to enroll Annie in pre-kindergarten, though, that same gloomy Catholic school's full-day schedule enticed me. I felt she needed more stimulation than I could provide at home, where play dates were hard to come by, and the lure of television was a constant temptation. She did well in this school's pre-kindergarten program, and there seemed no pressing need to switch her now. We also thought the smattering of religious education would be a bonus. It was by default, then, that we kept her at that Catholic school, a passive decision I still regret, a misstep that altered the course of Annie's life and thrust us both down a rabbit hole of misery. Yet what an exercise in maddening futility to ponder whether our lives would be so terribly different had we not overstayed our good run at that school and unleashed a torrent of lasting turmoil.

Chapter 1

> Ghost: An apparition of a dead person, which is
> believed to appear or become manifest to the living,
> typically as a nebulous image.
>
> *Oxford Dictionary*

"Ghosting," my therapist called my daughter's behavior that frigid February evening when I first confessed my horror over her clearly troubled state. The term ghosting sounds anachronistic now, of the pre-digital age when it referred to the shadows or secondary images seen on old-fashioned television screens, not the abrupt, cold vanishing of romantic partners we often hear about today. My therapist's metaphoric use of the term sounded chillingly appropriate back then, for when I looked at my daughter, I glimpsed an apparition of my former self, a disturbing replica of my own early anxiety. Just eight years old, Annie was riddled with morbid worries and irrational fears, scarcely resembling the vivacious scamp who once flitted through our house with glee. She no longer smiled or laughed or even cried. Her countenance was haunted, her features frozen in a mask of pitiful dread. I could hardly look into her frightened eyes without suffering pangs of heartache and inexplicable guilt. I stumbled through the days consumed by a suffocating sense of shame. This strange apprehension unhinged me, and eventually, the weight of it brought me to my knees.

But in truth, ominous signs had waxed and waned throughout Annie's earliest years. Often exuberant, she could also be deeply melancholy and intensely anxious. As a baby, she slept fitfully, almost always waking in a foul mood. By six months, she thrashed about and wailed with abandon as I changed her diaper, eclipsing the sweet moments of mother-baby gazing we once enjoyed. The slightest frustration elicited her blood-curdling screams, and her fevered tantrums frazzled me. She was exquisitely attuned to nuances of language, tonality, and emotion. At about nine months of age, when I serenaded her with "Rock-a-Bye-Baby," she cried and shook her head fiercely, as if she somehow grasped the fate of the baby in that precariously perched cradle.

The preschool years turned bleaker. I soon heard from most teachers that Annie seemed unhappy, but it was nothing anyone could put their finger on. At home, she frequently dwelled on the topic of death, mine as well as hers. The concept of Heaven held no comfort for her; it was *this world* she cared about, where she wanted us all to be together *forever*. During one of our daily walks, she spotted a dead squirrel lying in a neighbor's front yard. She pleaded with me to reassure her it would come back to life, to explain that it was not *really* dead. I dutifully attempted a rendering of the mythic rainbow bridge in the sky, which all the departed animals crossed over, but it fell flat on her grief-stricken ears. Bedtime reading, which usually soothed her, went terribly awry one night when Jack, the beloved dog in the Little House on the Prairie books, met an untimely death. Her despair was inconsolable, and she refused ever again to read from the

Ingalls family chronicles. After that traumatizing encounter, she screened all books, television shows, and movies for similar notes of impending disaster, determined to avoid another cataclysm of painful emotion. She also could not abide me listening to any "sad" music and was concerned when I was silent or meditative for any length of time. "What's the matter?" she would ask, which always struck me as unusually empathic in a child so young.

As Annie states:

Annie: *I was always an intensely anxious child. Often my mind got the best of me, and I was lost in a whirlwind of obsessive, paranoid thoughts. I worried about everything, especially about something happening to my family. The most distressing of all my worries was death. Some of my earliest memories are of haunting questions regarding the afterlife—what happens to us when we die? Where do we go? Are we surrounded by our loved ones? At times I found myself inconsolable with worry, sobbing until I was gasping for air, refusing to leave my mother's side. I hated not having any clear answers to my questions, and everyone's attempts to comfort me gave me no solace. I wanted hard facts to convince me.*

❋ ❋ ❋ ❋ ❋ ❋

When she was seven years old, and a second-grader in Catholic school, Annie's mental health was profoundly shaken. Her class was preparing for the sacraments of their First Holy Communion and First Confession that fall, and she spoke fondly of her new teacher, a Maria von Trapp-type singing nun who played guitar and seemed to nurture the children with parental warmth. When I visited the classroom, Sister Maria displayed impressive patience with her rambunctious charges, tying shoes on the fly, answering a potpourri of impromptu questions, and engaging the students in fun quizzes. But as the school year progressed, Sister's religious instruction took front and center stage. She often reinforced her teachings by expressing her views on politics and moral issues. The Democratic candidate for President at that time favored abortion rights, and Sister denounced him as a "baby killer." Annie was quiet when she came home from school that day, and when I asked if there was anything wrong, she timidly wondered, "Is John Kerry really a baby killer?" It was the first of Sister's many character assassinations, each one sending Annie into another tizzy of confusion and anxiety. However, it was Sister's moralistic probing that unsettled Annie the most, almost right out of the gate:

Annie: When I began second grade, there was a new teacher assigned to our school, a rosy-faced, middle-aged nun. Sister Maria's cheery attitude quickly earned the appreciation of my peers, and her smooth-talking ways solidified her acceptance with class parents. The first few days of our relationship as student and teacher went off without a hitch, and school was dismissed for the weekend. When Monday morning rolled around, Sister Maria asked us who had been at Sunday mass. This was the first time a formal public survey had ever been conducted, and up until then, I hadn't heard the question posed so pointedly. I could immediately feel my cheeks flush as most of my classmates' hands went up. I didn't like to stand out. A handful of my peers and I were in the minority of those who had not attended, and we were all shifting in our seats sheepishly. Sister Maria scanned the room, making a mental note of the perpetrators. When she got to me, however, I felt her eyes lock seconds longer than with anyone else. It was as if she sniffed the fear in me, the vulnerability, right from the start. I recall thinking I might have imagined the uncomfortable interaction, that maybe I was crazy, but in hindsight, that brief, chilling moment set the tone for the rest of the school year.

As part of the groundwork for First Confession, Sister had designed a lengthy questionnaire for her students to review with their parents each evening. The objective of the exercise was to monitor their developing conscience. Questions ranged from whether they had any impure thoughts, to whether their eyes had lingered on any unchaste images on television, to whether they had browsed any improper reading material. Annie's mind reeled as she ruminated on the significance of her every thought and action.

Her concerns about sin sounded reasonable at first, but they soon turned alarming as she fretted over the slightest transgression, real or imagined. "Bad choices" lurked every-where—had she intentionally or even inadvertently listened to inappropriate music or watched a less than wholesome television show? Had she ever lied, stolen anything, hurt anyone? She could never be sure because she could never stop doubting herself. While shopping with me in Kohl's one afternoon, she accidentally knocked over a delicate Christmas ornament. As I picked up the glass fragments, I told her that accidents like this happened all the time, that no one in the store would mind, but she was so terrified and racked with guilt that she agonized over it for weeks. When she learned that the janitor at her school had broken his arm, she anguished over whether the water she spilled in the cafeteria that day might have caused him to slip and fall. Whenever she chatted with classmates, she worried they might think she had uttered some insolent remark and repeated almost everything she said to make herself absolutely clear. She was tortured by the fear that she had committed some other yet-to-be-revealed crime, and to avoid being caught by the police, she brushed her hands back and forth over any surface she touched to wipe away her fingerprints.

Sister Maria had exhorted her pupils to seek God's forgiveness in their hearts and through the sacrament of Confession. All sinners, she said, especially unrepentant ones, would be punished by God and doomed to an eternity in Hell with the Devil, the most fearsome entity of all. Annie drank in everything Sister said. Mike and I tried our best to counter Sister's more extreme views, but Annie was never persuaded. She told us that she had asked Sister Maria what God would have done had the Devil himself said he was sorry, but Sister merely replied that the Devil would never have done such a thing. Eventually, I refused to review Sister's questionnaire with Annie and nearly shouted at her—"*I won't do this anymore! You haven't done anything seriously wrong in your entire young life. And God, if anything, is all about love, not fear and guilt!*"

The transformation that came over Annie in this short time was shocking. I noticed she was now constantly counting things with her fingers—the cracks in the walls, the books on the shelves, the sides of picture frames, anything her fearful eyes landed on. As I read to her at bedtime, her eyes scanned the room, and her fingers rippled beneath the blanket, still busy tallying. When I described her behavior to my therapist, he assumed she was counting the beads on the rosary, but it was impossible to imagine she was kneading those churchly artifacts, so redolent of religion and everything that frightened her. Years later, Annie told me she had never *decided* to count things but had just started doing it and then *had* to do it to ward off some future disaster. The mindless act of counting inanimate objects was emotionally numbing for her, keeping the tidal wave of anxiety temporarily at bay.

Annie: Second grade is a highly anticipated time in Catholic school. The year revolves around receiving your First

Holy Communion, an enormous event in your young life. It was the teacher's job to prepare us by ensuring we understood the "rules" of Christ, that we knew how to uphold the Ten Commandments, and had formally confessed our sins. I quickly noted Sister Maria was taking her preparation duties very seriously. When she spoke of religion, her face hardened, and her voice became solemn as she preached to us the importance of never, ever disobeying the commandments. She said that if we violated the commandments, it would make us sinners, and sinners do not receive First Holy Communion.

Over the course of the year, I found myself gradually unraveling. Sister Maria's incessant lectures regarding the high standards the Catholic Church held for leading a sacramental life and the endless list of sins one was capable of committing was overwhelming to me.

In November, Mike and I paid a visit to Sister Maria, the first in a series of disturbing confrontations. Sister appeared vaguely sympathetic at first, but then hinted at greater challenges to come as Annie hit puberty. I bristled at her knowing pronouncement. *Who was she to imply such things of my child? How would she know?* However, we appealed to her compassion and requested she soften her religious stance with Annie, perhaps even reach out to her in kindness. Her tepid response was unnerving, but we left that meeting still hopeful for improvement now that we had cleared the air.

We kept an uneasy vigil over our daughter and quickly realized that circumstances at school did not improve once we alerted Sister Maria to her troubles. We did not expect her to act as Annie's therapist, but we had anticipated at least a modicum of sensitivity toward her suffering. Sister was annoyed, though, by Annie's repeated hand-washing and other ritualistic behaviors, and a sinister acrimony came to mark their relationship. We could only surmise that Sister had taken umbrage to remarks we had made at our initial meeting. On the other hand, we were hesitant to believe everything Annie reported to us, wondering whether her extreme anxiety had distorted her perceptions. We scheduled a follow-up meeting with Sister as a reality check. This time I was too distressed to accompany Mike, but he brought Annie along as the barometer of truth. Sister denied nothing Annie told us and corroborated all the facts she had given us so far. When Mike's temper flared, and he demanded mercy toward our daughter, Sister shouted back at him, defending her God-given duty to uphold the Catholic teachings.

The parochial school Annie attended was small, with only one class per grade, so it was impossible to simply switch her to another class and change teachers. We considered the pros and cons of withdrawing her halfway through the school year, but decided instead to transfer her out in June when the change would feel more natural and less traumatic for her. As terrified as Annie was of Sister Maria, she was ambivalent about leaving the school and the friends she had made there. We were still hoping for some version of détente with Sister when a new development so infuriated us that we decided not only to stay the course, but to hold her accountable for her actions at the highest level.

Annie: I didn't want to leave my friends and be ripped away from my school and community, to start all over, alone, in a foreign place. Why should I be the one to leave?

Why must I be punished for her sins? I didn't ask to be targeted by this "servant of God." Up until then, I didn't know there was anything wrong with my existence. Why didn't the school recognize the crime of this adult in a position of power, bullying a seven-year-old child?

I wanted to stay with my friends. They were all I had

left. I couldn't speak. The words wouldn't come. I was paralyzed by fear.

At the halfway mark in the school year, when parents were polled on whether our children would be returning in September for another year, I sent Sister Maria a letter informing her that Annie would not be returning. Her mental health was now at stake, I wrote, and in the scheme of things, took precedence over a Catholic education. On the heels of that letter, Sister announced to the class that Annie, as well as her parents, was having a problem accepting the Catholic teachings, and thus, she would not be eligible to receive communion with the rest of the class in the spring. When she was out of earshot of the other children, Sister taunted Annie with whispered warnings about the fires of Hell that awaited heathens like us. Mike and I were outraged and swore we would not allow such cruelty to stand. Determined to exact justice at any cost from the principal, the pastor, and the entire Catholic Church, if need be, we hunkered down for a protracted battle. Had it not been at the expense of our already broken daughter, it might all have been worth it.

Chapter 2

Methinks I hear, methinks I see,
Ghosts, goblins, fiends; my phantasy
Presents a thousand ugly shapes,
Headless bears, and apes,
Doleful outcries, and fearful sights,
My sad and dismal soul affrights.

The Anatomy of Melancholy, Robert Burton

By December, Annie was in the throes of full-blown obsessive-compulsive disorder (OCD), a condition that causes individuals to doubt the truth of their own experiences. Every thought, spoken word, action, and sensory intake is examined in excruciating detail. "You can't trust your ordinary good judgment, can't trust your eyes that see no dirt, or *really* believe that the door is locked. You know you have done nothing harmful, but in spite of this good sense, you must go on checking and counting," writes Dr. Judith Rapoport in *The Boy Who Couldn't Stop Counting*. Most people with OCD also have "obsessions," unwanted intrusive thoughts, images, or urges that trigger intensely distressing feelings. In his book, *Tormenting Thoughts & Secret Rituals: The Hidden Epidemic of Obsessive-Compulsive Disorder*, Dr. Ian Osborn states that obsessions are "usually the worst thoughts that you could ever imagine. They do not in any way represent who you are ... the truth is most people get unwanted thoughts." Yet where most people recognize the ludicrous and baseless nature of these thoughts and then turn their attention elsewhere, individuals with OCD "become horrified by these thoughts and try to fight them, and by doing so make them worse" (Osborn). Fear fuels the obsessions, adds Dr. Osborn; "Somehow, in the mind, fearing a thought exaggerates the importance of that thought, guaranteeing that it will return again and again. Fearing unacceptable thoughts turns them into obsessions."

To soothe their anxiety, OCD sufferers adopt behaviors called "compulsions" or "rituals"—Annie's counting and fingerprint-wiping, for example—to help distract the mind and alleviate the distressing feelings. Without the distracting compulsions, the individual experiences a feeling of impending doom. OCD thoughts and fears can strike haphazardly, or they can be intimately linked to developmental stages in one's life. Annie's obsessions were imbued with the element of "scrupulosity," a form of OCD in which the primary anxiety is the fear of guilt over some perceived religious or moral failure. Her fears of displeasing God and going to Hell compelled her to weigh everything she said, read, watched, wore, or thought on the harshest scales of her conscience. The psychological pain of OCD is often described as "torturous."

According to the National Institute of Mental Health, approximately 2.3 percent of the population between the ages of 18-54 suffers from OCD; that is, one person out of fifty is affected by some form of obsession or compulsion. And one out of every one hundred children is diagnosed with OCD. The causes of the disorder are believed to range from the deeply psychoanalytic to the purely biological. Psychotherapist Steven Levenkron, in his book, *Obsessive-Compulsive Disorder: Treating and Understanding Crippling Habits,* maintains that "in an obsessive-compulsive individual, the seeds of vulnerability may be sown during the first four years of life, for it is during this period that bonding between mother and child takes place. The seeds may also precede birth in the form of a constitutional (hereditary) predisposition to anxiety and/or depression." Another leading or predisposing factor can be some form of consistent environmental stress. Yet, even when all these influences are present, "OCD symptoms often await a trauma before emerging" (Levenkron).

٭ ٭ ٭ ٭ ٭ ٭

In 1853, Charles Dickens captured the ease with which obsessions and rituals can fold into the fabric of one's life. In the novel *Bleak House,* Esther Summerson, the warm-hearted protagonist and ward of a noble benefactor, believes herself an orphan until she discovers her mother is very much alive, an aristocrat of sterling reputation whom she already knows. When her mother finally reveals her identity, she swears Esther to secrecy because of the scandalous details surrounding her birth. Here Esther describes the psychological toll this took on her:

> *"... I could not always conquer that terror of myself which had seized me when I first knew the secret. At no time did I dare to utter her name. I felt as if I did not even dare to hear it. If the conversation anywhere, when I was present, took that direction, as it sometimes naturally did, I tried not to hear it—I mentally counted, repeated something that I knew, or went out of the room. I am conscious, now, that I often did these things when there can have been no danger of her being spoken of; but I often did them in the dread I had of hearing anything that might lead to her betrayal, and to her betrayal through me."*

Esther's worries did not exist solely in her imagination as Annie's did, and she did not fear the agonies of hell if her mother's identity were revealed, but her anxiety propelled along the same tracks Annie's did. For good reason, Esther avoided her mother's name; grave consequences would ensue were she to drop her guard. Yet that excessive anxiety, groundless or not, strains the mental faculties and sometimes generates obsessive-compulsive behaviors.

Chapter 3

> "There was such a horror of him, and such a
> perception of my own merely momentary
> discrepancy from him, that it was as if something
> hitherto solid within my breast gave way entirely,
> and I became a mass of quivering fear."

The Varieties of Religious Experience, William James

When I arrived at my therapist's door for our first session, I was in a state of subdued hysteria, the months leading up to it having been a private agony. I worked at that time as a medical transcriptionist alongside three other women whose desks were only a few feet from mine in a claustrophobic basement office. Though the work itself had once challenged me with its arcane terminology, the language had long since become rote. Sometimes the monotonous rhythm of doctors' dictation and typing for hours on end soothed me, but more often, it was stultifying, leaving me copious amounts of time to ruminate on my own thoughts, which usually focused on Annie. Her desperate plight had somehow become my own. As she disappeared behind that mask of fear, I, too, lost my bearings and all sense of self. The anxiety that hounded her poured into the interstices of my own fragile psyche until I was stunned into a profound state of unrest. The more preoccupied I was with her trials, the more embroiled I was in my own stew of emotions and the less able I was to help her when she needed me most.

In the office, I willed myself to remain as outwardly calm as possible. I was not accustomed to sharing my troubles, and the strain of suppressing my emotions amid those chatty women was intensely stressful. To keep from complete self-implosion, now and then I let off steam by disclosing some morsel of Annie's difficulties, though it was all I could do to sound nonchalant, as if I were only marginally concerned about her. I deliberated over whether to tell my supervisor that I was dealing with a personal difficulty and thus might seem a little off at work, but the last thing I wanted to do was call attention to myself. Despite my efforts to remain poised, cracks began to mar the facade. One coworker offered me Ativan to calm my jagged nerves. Another told me of her mother's mental collapse after a break with the Catholic Church. I girded myself not to identify too closely with this woman's tale of religious disillusionment or betray any revealing dismay over her mother's years-long recovery.

As time went on, the pressure of hiding the peculiar circumstances of my crisis depleted me. My life at that time had taken on an agitated, even mournful aspect. Midlife ennui enervated me, and I sometimes sat in a languorous haze, unsure of my next footstep. I had neglected—been afraid, really—to plan for the second half of my life's journey, the part that would force me beyond the safe confines of my familiar domestic routines. Mostly full-time parenting had sheltered me from my deeper, more troubled self, the one I kept avoiding as I preoccupied myself with family matters. With Joe in high school and Annie in grade school, I felt increasingly useless and ill at ease. My discomfort was at first mildly disconcerting, like suddenly walking unencumbered after pushing a baby carriage for many years, but eventually, it was debilitating, as a loathsome nervousness pervaded my very being. Bouts of depression and panic had felled me in the past, and various odd and stressful symptoms broke out periodically, but the darkness that enveloped me at this stage was prolonged and crippling. And now, during Annie's abominable second-grade school year, it was drastically exacerbated by my anxiety over her horrendous mental suffering.

I recognized and identified with Annie's fears to such an extreme degree that she may as well have been a ghost, the ghost of my suppressed emotional past. I knew *exactly* how she felt because I, too, had suffered from obsessive-compulsive disorder for many of my early years, yet when she began manifesting its symptoms, in a frenzy of denial I rushed to convince myself that although *she* might be troubled, *I* was still okay. The obsessive thoughts, the rituals, the counting, this was all *her* stuff, not mine, I told myself. I once even shamed her by protesting, "You're a strong girl; *just stop!*" as if it were in her power to banish such madness at will. I could not bear to acknowledge how much she suffered, how deeply I, too, had once suffered. I wanted only to turn away from that frightful image, but now the evidence that Annie had absorbed my woeful essence was indisputable and eviscerated me.

The fact that I cowered from this ghost in my own home smacked of such personal failure, I could hardly summon the courage to engage with people. I was overcome with the most hideous anxiety and could scarcely move, think, or speak. No one knew this other version of me. How would I admit to it now? And how would we rescue Annie? What would that even look like? What if she needed medication? Though I had spent most of my life hampered by varying degrees of anxiety, I never received any professional help of my own. Who even talked about "anxiety" back then, and who knew there was help for it? In fact, it was not until what William Styron calls the "manifest crisis" of my daughter's suffering that my protective shell split open, suspending me in a state of pure existential terror. There finally came a day as I sat in that office, barely able to strike a key on my computer, that I inwardly declared I could no longer live in such abject fear and trembling.

Immediately upon arriving home from work, I combed the "yellow pages" for psychologists, mental health offices, anyone who might save me from myself, from the ghost. Several receptionists offered up appointments weeks or months in the future. *No; don't you see? I don't have the luxury of time. I may not make it until tomorrow!* I wanted to shout. There was one psychologist who quickly returned my call and offered to see me for therapy that same evening. When he inquired into the nature of my problem, my throat constricted with anxiety, and I could hardly get two words out. I felt lightheaded, unable to hear, and could not concentrate on what he said, but something he mentioned about the tendency of the unconscious to erupt when important life issues are ignored registered with me.

By the time I finally sought this help, I dreaded waking up each morning. With the first flicker of consciousness, the vise of terror gripped me and never let up. Even in sleep, I sensed a sickening miasma. I was so nauseated with panic I could no longer taste food and noticed my clothes hanging off my now thin frame. My chest contracted with unbearable apprehension, and my always latent social anxiety blossomed into a bizarre phobia. In company, I blushed fiercely with self-consciousness for no apparent reason and sometimes choked embarrassingly on my spoken words. I was afraid of people, even those I loved, as their wholesome faces highlighted my own unnatural feelings of disintegration. I wished I were invisible or could permanently disguise myself, for the sensation of being looked at filled me with a tremendous dread, as if someone might peer into the depths of my freakish soul and feel sorry for the poor fool I had become. The rational part of me was demoralized by my paranoia, but the adrenaline never stopped pumping through my body, always on high alert to the danger of panic situations. Everywhere I went, I planned an escape route so that I could run from anyone whose eyes paused too long on my sad, tense face. The tumult in my mind so discomposed me that I sometimes had the sensation of being physically dissociated from my body, as if I were observing my pathetically neurotic self from a distance.

I had been trying to spare my husband the spectacle of my undoing for some time, but before leaving home that night, I finally proclaimed to him in tears that I was "falling apart" and that I was "going for help" at that very moment. The words *"I'm ashamed, so ashamed"* kept tumbling out of my mouth, though I could not say what it was I was ashamed *of*, and his concern at my frightening state of mind shamed me even more. Somehow the idea of seeing a therapist had never entirely impressed itself upon me, but now I knew my life depended on it.

I told my therapist in that initial phone call that the anxiety I suffered from was "social," and he took care that first night not to look directly at me, only to glance at me now and then from an angle. But he was easy to talk to and a good listener, and despite my nervousness, the details of my story began rapidly unspooling—my heartache over Annie, my strange sense of guilt, my emotional breakdown. As we spoke, he scribbled things on a large white pad with markers, like a quick-sketching caricature artist. Toward the end of the session, he held up the pad to show me a diagram filled with colorful words, phrases, and swirls, which represented an intelligible whole to him, a coherent summary of everything we talked about. While the biting winds whipped about his office, I listened as he recapped our discussion, and when he mentioned the word "ghosting," I knew instantly he hit the mark. History had sadly, regrettably, repeated itself, and that one session was like a logjam bursting in my psyche, precipitating a cascade of emotion and insight.

Chapter 4

"The journey through madness is essentially an
individual one. We can only share part of that
journey with others; the greatest part of the journey
is ours and ours alone."

Recovery: An Alien Concept, Ron Coleman

Before starting therapy, my sense of guilt over Annie's troubles was profound but amorphous. I detested myself for her loss of innocence and the agony of her OCD nightmare; I reproached myself as if I had intentionally perpetrated against her the most grievous of crimes, but I could not articulate it in plain language because I had never come to terms with it in myself. I lamented to my husband that I could deal with anything, any physical affliction in my child, only not this dastardly behavior, not this contemptible ghost of anxiety. The children must never know where it came from, I had insisted; they must never suspect I was responsible for its presence in our midst.

Though I presented with the chief complaint of an overriding concern for my daughter, my therapist reminded me that *I* was the patient here, not *her*. For his purposes, *mine* was the injured psyche in need of emergency care. "We need to get *you* well before you can be of help to your daughter," he said. He was skilled and probed the subterranean tissues of my mind deftly, wondering what my "family of origin" was like, what was going on in the marriage, what our parenting styles were like, and why the need for a Catholic education for our daughter. He promised that with more understanding of our family dynamics and more effective parenting techniques, Annie's symptoms would most likely disappear. His prognosis sounded hopeful, but improbable to me. He downplayed the possibility that Annie had inherited a physiological predisposition to OCD, infinitely more curious about the generational legacies of shame buried beneath my family tree. I disagreed and challenged him. *But what of the long genetic strands my daughter had inherited from me, predisposing her to the darker side of life? What about that ghost, my wretched doppelganger? Wasn't all this just regrettable genetic loading, the product of my lousy neurological wiring?*

I later recalled that just days before phoning my therapist, I professed to my husband while glancing through some family photographs that I could no longer bear to look at them, for they filled me with a bewildering sadness. It was not until years later that I recognized that echo of grief from my mother, who had secreted away her own family's photographs, the same ones that heartened me with tidings that I might have had a happy childhood that I once burrowed cozily in the hub of a large bustling family. My brothers and I often attempted to recover those photos, but my mother always rebuffed us. It was only after her death that we reclaimed them and became reacquainted with our younger selves; me, the smiling five-year-old in the lemon-yellow chiffon dress surrounded by four brothers. I still remember the rainy spring evening my mother sent my older brother out to pick up that dress from the avenue store so I would have it in time for

Easter.

When I gaze upon those pictures today, I imagine it was the sight of those five innocent children in their unperturbed beauty that haunted my mother, for there were unsuspected vulnerabilities at play, inconceivable tragedies to come. Those snapshots might have evoked flashbacks of an earlier joy too piercing to her heart. Perhaps she was oppressed by sorrow for the troubled lives they would lead, filled with regret for the inevitable mistakes she had made. My empathy with her now may have had its seeds planted in that deep-rooted female tendency to blame ourselves, or maybe our brain chemistries so closely aligned that our responses to life's stresses were uncannily similar, or maybe I so thoroughly inherited or internalized her faintly melancholy disposition that depression was my birthright.

During our early sessions, when my therapist asked what my mother had been like, I proudly told him, "A saint!" but he looked at me quizzically as if to say, *"Oh? Surely there must be more to it than that."* I was annoyed and felt protective of my personal history. Later, he went on to imply that I might have played a more active role in the manifestation of my daughter's symptoms than merely transmitting my shoddy genes. Was he trying to provoke me? I wondered. I was flummoxed as he inferred that my situation might not be all that surprising. When he pressed me on—*Could I not think of anything besides my genetic inheritance, my daughter's inborn temperament, and her strict Catholic indoctrination that might be part of this equation? Might there be ways that my husband and I had welcomed the ghost into our home?*—I could not imagine what he meant. *What did Annie's symptoms have to do with my behavior? I told you all I know, especially about my crappy genes and the terrible vulnerability I imposed upon my daughter, remember?!* I felt he was accusing me of something even more terrible than I had already acknowledged. He delivered this query in the last moments of our session when there was no time to "process" it. Another client was waiting, and as I rose from the couch and walked slowly toward the door, disturbing new impressions crowded in. *Were my husband and I part of the problem? Was it not only Sister Maria who harmed her, but were we, too, responsible for Annie's fears and overwhelming anxiety?*

By the time I reached home that night, I was flooded with discomfiting thoughts. The suspicion that we had been repressing Annie in small but significant ways flabbergasted me, but then it somehow rang true. Against the grain of her fiery creative spirit, we set stringent rules about music, clothes, and television. But had we quashed that exciting bohemian streak? Her fierce temper tested our restraint, but had we damaged her with too much discipline? The idea that we were stifling our daughter jarred me, and then it hurt me, but as its disturbing ramifications sank in, it devastated me. *What had we been so afraid of, and why did this revelation so unsettle me?*

My shameful biology was no longer the culprit here; there was something about *me, personally,* that was at fault. This new mortification stung deep, engulfing me in untold revulsion for myself. *Wait a minute, though ... was most of this really about me? Was I the one who was repressed? Was it my own wild nature I was afraid of, not Annie's?* I was disgusted by my willful blindness and felt there was no end to the misery I spread. I berated myself again and again, *owned it* all, personalized every last bit of it.

I had broached the topic of medication with my therapist only once, early on. He assured me he knew of a psychiatrist who could prescribe me something, but he also added that medication sometimes backfired by masking a patient's symptoms and underlying problems. I was hesitant to take medication, anyway, wary of it and tainted by the idea that resorting to it somehow indicated I was weak, not equipped to handle life. He said what I wanted to hear, and therefore, although I felt I might pass out with fright at any moment, I decided to be a "good" patient and soldier on without it.

And those first therapy sessions were exhilaratingly cathartic as I quickly reaped the benefits of the intimate therapeutic relationship. My husband was relieved and listened late into the night as I confronted the past and connected the dots of my family's emotional history. Between weekly sessions, our therapy room discussions reverberated in my mind, sometimes sending electric currents of insight through the depths of my being. I was tapping into unexplored sides of myself, discovering influences that had forged my personality; however, along with all that bracing self-knowledge came a terrible sadness for the untended recesses of my heart. This was not a loving self-compassion, but a lonely and immeasurable sorrow for my own self. I grieved for all the bittersweet what-might-have-beens and glimpsed the countless bright turns my life might have taken had I been a bolder person.

As the months passed, I struggled to regain my equilibrium. For all the progress I had made in therapy, I did not *feel* any better. In fact, my anxiety intensified, and I was panicked with the thought that I might truly be going insane. I was taking evening graduate courses at that time at Villanova University, having decided, two years prior, that a return to the classroom would help scratch the itch of my midlife restlessness. My goal was a second master's degree, this time in "liberal studies," where I had ample freedom to pursue my own interests. I was about halfway through the program, focusing on philosophy courses, when Annie and I fell to pieces. I was enrolled in a survey of American Philosophers and looked forward to delving into William James's classic *The Varieties of Religious Experience*, but as my distress deepened,

I could no longer concentrate on my reading or complete the assignments. Additionally, we were learning about James's "sick souls," those sensitive, despairing individuals he wrote about so trenchantly, and I was mortified by how similar my saturnine spirits were to theirs. These were the same souls who later experienced ecstatic visions, contributed greatly to our understanding of human nature, and performed selfless humanitarian works, but I was abashed and tried to drop the class. My professor advised me to take a grade of "Incomplete" and rest through the summer. I had never taken an Incomplete grade before, but he said, "it was not the end of the world" and trusted I would get the work done by the fall semester. And then, for the first time in my life, I had a serious car accident after rashly pulling out into the "suicide" lane of traffic along a busy thoroughfare. A young family was involved, and I thanked God no one was hurt, but again I was overcome with guilt and shame. *"Maybe the accident was not solely your fault,"* my therapist said. *"Maybe the other car pulled into the lane too early."* But I could not quite remember checking my rearview mirror, a blunder I considered egregious and indefensible.

By summer, I entered the most agonizing passage of my journey, the stage at which, as William Styron articulated in *Darkness Visible,* "I first became fully aware that the struggle with the disorder in my mind—a struggle which had engaged me for several months—might have a fatal outcome." My mood was so low and I was so agitated that I descended into an underworld of unceasing gloom. My sensibilities had recalibrated to a more somber pitch, and I was attuned to the timbre of sadness everywhere I went. My usual taste in music was too tender for my aching emotions. Only raucous strains could fleetingly blot out the mental pain. Television, movies, books, most of life, in fact, seemed inconsequential compared to my own doleful situation. I was not the sort to escape into drugs or alcohol; I was, as a matter of course, stone-cold sober. My only relief came from reading the works of authors who had struggled with similar mental infirmities because they made me feel less alone and gave me hope that I, too, might survive and one day recover.

In a coffee shop with my husband one evening, I observed a group of what appeared to be "disturbed" adults on an outing with their "caretakers." A handsome, seemingly distraught young man at one point put his head down on the table as if the torment in his mind were too much to bear, and the commiseration I felt with him took my breath away. He may simply have been tired or overstimulated, but to me, it was as though all the mental agony in the universe were being revealed and I recognized and understood the darkest shadows in each person's heart.

My therapist ventured with me to the many murky corners of my psyche, but I offered my stricken soul selectively, hating to appear desperate, deranged, or pitifully far gone. And therefore, he never asked, *"Are you still in terrible psychological pain? Are you feeling paranoid about yourself? Do you ever think about dying? Are you suicidal?"* He could not know that thoughts of death possessed me now, even comforted me and that an odious paranoia warped my perceptions. I could not be certain *who* I was. In that solipsistic void, all the guilt, shame, and self-hatred metastasized into looming fantasies, and I feared I might be someone even more horrible than I had already imagined. I told my husband that the woman he used to know was gone, that he was now living with the ghost, who might say or do anything, who might at any moment shame him or the children in some outrageous, unpredictable way. It was as if some savage beast was pounding on the doors of my psyche to be let in, and with the last of my strength, I fought against it.

I envied the seemingly well-adjusted masses around me

and longed to trade places even with my beloved pets, for I imagined their existence harbored none of the psychic pain I endured. Although I knew there was a devoted husband and children who loved me, a compassionate therapist who cared about me, and loyal friends and family ready with encouraging words, the bounds of my suffering had surpassed comprehensible human proportions, and it was impossible for me to either convey or rise above it. The span of a lifetime struck me as intolerably long; where I once woke in the night frantic at the thought of my dwindling years, I now yearned to leap over them in order that my agony might mercifully end. I rationalized to my husband that it would be better for everyone were I not around; he would be all right, I insisted, but it was the children I could not bear to traumatize.

I felt so utterly self-conscious every second of waking life and longed for oblivion. I was exhausted by the monumental effort it took to place one foot in front of the other, and I prayed that God might somehow intervene on my behalf and inflict some incurable malady that would take me, quickly, for I knew I could not carry out such destruction on my own. *"Just take me, God, please take me!"* I prayed.

Chapter 5

> "'Stepping into the unknown' means turning to face
> what we have been struggling against, the suffering
> that is our experience of mortal woundedness,
> and allowing ourselves to descend into the core
> of such experience."
>
> *Mortally Wounded, Michael Kearney*

In the meantime, I did the only thing I could do, tried to get hold of my emotions through therapy. I knew that the memories of every childhood were filtered through an idiosyncratic lens and that the reflections and experiences of two family members can diverge more than they coincide, but it was incumbent on me now not to turn away from the past.

I was not an easy child. I knew that I had made it hard for anyone to feel close to me, but I had no doubt that in my earliest years, I was loved and coddled by my parents and was "securely attached," as they say. But after those years, I can only remember being miserable and overcome with frightening anger that estranged me from my family as well as myself. For most of my young life, I remained emotionally cut off from both parents, which I assumed was because I pushed them away with my ill temper. They were at a loss with how to govern me and, as a result, kept their distance. I tried to subdue my explosive personality on my own, but in the process of suppressing so much emotion, I became trapped inside myself. I forgot how to be real and spontaneous, how to connect with my family other than in the most lifeless, detached way. I withdrew into a protective cocoon and never admitted to anyone I was bursting at the seams with anxiety. I did not even know there was a word for what I felt.

At home, I was mostly irritable and uncommunicative, which could not have been pleasant for my parents. As I got older and eventually moved out of the house, I told myself it was best to forget those awkward years, though at the same time, they felt like an atrocity I would one day need to answer for. In time I learned to work within my social limitations, curating a deep but avoidant personality, eschewing the extrovert's life and any of the more outgoing activities that would betray me. I kept my ambitions low and hid behind my shy exterior. Early in my marriage, I felt the need to explain to my husband the troubled child and young person I had been, but he dismissed it and said whatever I had been like then only made me the person he loved today. So I dropped the topic and tried to be as normal and well-adjusted as he was.

* * * * * *

I was a child in the '6os, the era of laissez-faire parenting, particularly for most fathers who stayed primarily in the background while the mothers did the lion's share of heavy lifting. As kids, we went "out to play," all day, our parents none the wiser as to what we did or where we went. My father, a New York City policeman, related better to my four brothers, and my mother had her hands full with my more demanding siblings. I must have naturally hung back, as I still do, never pushing for more attention than I got, which was a boon to my harried mother. I knew she cared passionately about us in her understated way, supportive and concerned with the daily goings-on in our lives, sympathizing with us deeply when we were sick or bothered in any way. Her love was so powerful that it was healing just to think of her, but back then, I always felt somehow apart from her. We were also not a physically close family, with easy displays of affection, but then again, this may only be *my* recollection, revealing my *own* aversion to family intimacy. My therapist once described my parents' noninterfering style as "benign neglect," an oxymoronic term I liked because it captured both my mother's saintly but un-demonstrative love as well as my father's confusing remote-ness.

My mother was our quiet, unassuming matriarch. Though she claimed to be "a melancholic," we did not think of her as depressive. She was thoughtful and introspective but not given to brooding; she was too busy and practical for that, more comfortable looking outward than inward. Highly intelligent, she read voraciously from the stack of books at her bedside. She was also keenly interested in politics and the state of the world, poring over several magazines and newspapers each day, including the *New York Times*. Not in the least athletic herself, she took an interest in sports so she could discuss them with her sports-minded children. She identified with the troubled, the unfortunate, and the weak and was just plain *nice* to everyone.

When I became a parent myself, I looked at my mother with a new appreciation for all she had experienced. The moody sullenness of my younger years had dispersed in early adulthood, and we were cultivating a more satisfying rela-tionship. My joys doubled when shared with her. She was easy to be around and never criticized my bumbling parenting skills or offered unsolicited advice; rather, she only encouraged me while basking in the joys of first-time grandparenthood. She had suffered mild post-partum blues with each of her five children but promised that for most women, it was a quickly passing phase. I somehow managed to dodge those hormonal tremors, but she made sure to check in with me, anyway. Though I had never held a baby before my son was born, the uncomplicated vulnerability of infancy moved me, and with my mother's steady guidance, I took to the job as if I had been waiting for it all my life. She died before Annie was born, but it seemed destined I would have a girl, manifesting her same slightly protruding lower lip and chocolate brown eyes. And in that eerie way that infants' sage expressions sometimes do, Annie invoked her spirit and seemed to link the three of us in an ethereal female bond.

If there were melancholy threads running through my mother's personality, they stemmed in part from her childhood. She had not been well-loved by her own mother. A dutiful, deferential daughter, I knew it saddened her that she could never please her mother or behold a gleam of pride in the older woman's eyes. Telephone calls between the two could send my mother into a funk for days until my father kidded her out of it. She was laid so low throughout her life by my grandmother's consistently withering criticism that the belief in her own inadequacy formed the bedrock of her being.

My mother was often confounded by a recurring dream she had of an abandoned baby crying in an empty room. Each time she had it, she exclaimed, *"I had the dream again! I just can't figure out who that baby is!"* She wondered if it might have been her second child, an extremely mellow infant who slept through most of his first year. Or maybe it was one of the other children whose distress she had failed to notice. Years after my mother's death, while driving home from work one day, the thought occurred to me that *she* was that baby. *Of course! She* was the one who had needed her mother's loving attention, the infant whose cries for comfort and validation were ignored throughout her life.

My mother was an early proponent of The Hemlock Society, one of the country's first assisted-suicide organizations, because she feared the prolonged physical suffering of death; however, when she lay dying from cancer, it was the mental straits of suffering that toppled her. Her existential fear of the unknown was prodigious, and she despaired that no one would be waiting to greet her in the afterlife. She did not feel important enough to anyone who had preceded her in death to have that privilege, not even her own mother. Though she found deep and abiding love with my father, the fact that she missed out on the major bond that forms us always pained me. What I most admired about her, though, was her ability to behave in a way so radically different from the template she was given, a triumph that seems to me now like breaking free after being encased in a large block of cement.

She was in her early sixties and had just retired from a long career as a bank teller when she received the news that she had a rare and fatal bile duct tumor. From the moment she heard the diagnosis, she began slowly retreating from us as she struggled to come to terms with her life. She abhorred the idea of becoming a burden to her children or the object of anyone's pity. She wanted desperately to make her peace with God, but in the end, her Catholic faith could not sustain her. Her children's love and her husband's unfailing devotion were the only things that mattered. She tried many times to tell us how pleased she was with us, how we had been the perfect son or daughter, to leave us without guilt. I shied away from these declarations—only *she* found the courage to say the things that needed to be said. After her death, my father found a pocket-sized diary she secretly kept during this period to take stock of her life. The last entries in that little white book were statements of her love for us, acknowledgments of each child and especially my father, demonstrating how well she knew us, saw us, and cherished us.

For the next several months, while my father tended to her every need, she receded deeper and deeper into herself. Soon she spoke of helicopters circling her apartment, authorities seeking to arrest her for a bank heist she was involved in, though she was puzzled why she could not remember it. She was besieged by other outlandish fears, and no amount of reassurance could put her mind at ease. Honest and guileless to a fault, she was the last person anyone who knew her would suspect of committing a crime. A few weeks later, the bridge to reality gave out, and she suffered a complete mental collapse.

Upon visiting her at home, we typically found her in bed, curled in the fetal position, with vacant, frightened eyes riveted somewhere in the distance. Her physical and mental condition deteriorated until my father could no longer care for her on his own. We committed her to a psychiatric institution directly across the street from her medical hospital, and she was shuttled back and forth between the two through an underground tunnel. At the psychiatric facility, they kept a suicide watch on her and attempted a brief, futile series of ECT treatments. While she lay shell-shocked in her room, we bore her gifts, brought new babies to rest at her side, and played her favorite Bing Crosby tunes on a cassette player on her nightstand, but she never emerged from that tomblike stillness.

An organic etiology such as stroke or metastasis could possibly explain my mother's mental condition, but I made meaning of it then, and still do now, without recourse to physiology. Her psychiatrist diagnosed her symptoms as "psychotic depression," a severe form that manifests with features like paranoia, delusions, and hallucinations. We knew that her psychological state was at variance with the mother we had always known, yet to me, it felt like an almost rational response to crushing misery, fear, and loss. I knew that for her, ironically, a psychotic break was the only way she could cope. Amid all that pain, she had finally needed to close the curtain and let the rest take its course.

I consider my mother's inward struggle to confront death as the "hero's journey." The hope is that this dangerous voyage will bestow spiritual blessings upon the individual, that she will emerge transformed, with some beneficial shift in consciousness; for my mother, say, a tranquil soul in the face of death. The internal crossing occurs at an unfathomable depth, and not everyone who attempts the passage can withstand its perils. Though my mother never enjoyed the hero's homecoming, I will always consider her attempt to reach that foreign shore profoundly brave.

* * * * * *

Since my mother's death, I have missed her unparalleled sympathy and support, but I am not certain that during the troubled years I write about here, I could have expressed my distress even to her. Just as I had stopped confiding in my father when Annie was in second grade, because I did not want to dampen his delight in her, I might have done the same with my mother. I would not have wanted either of them to know how disturbed Annie really was or how close to madness the ghost was driving me. They had been through enough in their own lives, and I felt they finally deserved some peace.

Chapter 6

> "Depression leads him close to the wounds, but only
> the mourning for what he has missed, missed at the
> crucial time, can lead to real healing."
>
> *The Drama of the Gifted Child, Alice Miller*

I was not particularly close to any of my siblings growing up, but one of my brothers, Jimmy, was not quite a year older than I was—"Irish twins," they called us—and in many ways embodied my complete foil. Where I kept my distance, he clung to both parents, especially my mother. Where I was self-contained and reticent, he was disruptive and kept little to himself. Where he was hyperactive, I was outwardly calm. While he faithfully kissed my mother goodnight every evening, I barely acknowledged her as the lights went down. I outperformed him academically and beat him in most of the games we played, while he chafed at the constraints of school and was a touchy sore loser. He manifested mental health problems early, OCD and depression, while I suffered privately, hiding my symptoms from everyone. Jimmy learned, though, to channel some of his volatile moodiness and energy to achieve minor fame in our neighborhood as a superior athlete and basketball star. He also possessed an innocence and eagerness to please, which escaped me. The essence of his personality was *good* and childlike, while the story I came to believe about myself was that, in contrast to him, I was somehow *bad*.

One day in my early twenties, I was emboldened to ask my mother why she had not tried to draw me out when I was a child, why she had not engaged with me more. It was the first time I ever alluded to such matters, and it was as if I had just knocked the wind out of her. I told her I had suffered in my baffling isolation, but she said she had not been aware I was particularly anxious or troubled. I knew that in her kindness, she had tried to give me privacy amid the flock of boys in our small apartment and probably hoped I would outgrow my ornery disposition. She did her best with all of us, but at that stage in my life, I realized I had wanted more. Part of me understood how unfair it was to hold her responsible for deciphering the mysteries of my soul, but another part of me, the angry, sulking child hiding in her room, rued the fact that she had simply been left alone.

Then my mother said something unexpected—"*I withdrew into myself during those years. Nothing was ever the same after the shooting.*" It was a pivotal event in our family's history. I was six years old at the time, and my two oldest brothers were thirteen and eleven. They sometimes hung around in the same crowd of friends; Billy, a thrill-seeker, as my mother said, was the unofficial leader of the pack, while Paul, the younger brother, was more easy-going and happier to follow along. On a summer afternoon when their group had indulged in some underage drinking at the park, Billy instigated an argument with a rival gang of young teens. The two clans agreed to meet up later that night at one of the boys' homes. There were no parents present at the boy's house that night, and when the earlier altercation resumed, the host took down his father's loaded rifle from a rack on the wall and shot and killed one of their closest friends. The boys all ran for cover, but the shooter caught Billy as he crouched under a chair, pinning him to the floor with the tip of the rifle. *"You're next, Billy!"* he shouted, but then seconds later, he raised the gun, allowing him to escape into the night with the rest of the boys.

It was a singular evening for all of us. Sometime after dinner, my mother must have received a phone call from my father, who was at work that night, and then hustled my other two brothers and me into a taxicab, which was such a striking curiosity that if for no other reason, I would have remembered the night for that alone. The four of us driving through the dark city streets seemed an adventure at first, until we arrived at an intimidating-looking building that turned out to be our local police station. I was confused to see my father waiting outside for us. Inside the building, I watched as my parents huddled with several police officers in a series of private conversations. I heard the word "shot" several times, which scared me. Neither of them told us what was going on, but I breathed in and stored up the illicit nature of that trauma as if I, too, were somehow complicit in a crime.

As time passed, I deduced enough of the story to figure out that a friend of Billy and Paul had been shot and killed at a party they attended, but that neither brother pulled the trigger, a great relief to me. After this event, a pall seemed to settle over our home, as if each of us had internalized the shame of that night. The immediacy of the episode eventually faded, but the memory of it could be powerfully recalled in an instant. I can remember only one time in my life being confronted about the shooting; otherwise, I never mentioned it. As I played with a group of kids in the hallway of our apartment building, my best friend's sister stated out of the blue that she knew my brothers *"were at the shooting."* I panicked and blurted out, *"But they didn't do it!"* Embarrassed and galled at having to defend my brothers, I was also troubled by an odd sense of guilt. *Maybe someone in my house really was guilty,* I thought. *Why is she saying this to me? Does she know something I don't know? I feel like I did something wrong, too!*

My parents had no doubt tried to protect us younger children by not talking about the shooting, but the incident festered in my mind. For years I was steeped in nebulous guilt. When I was nearly out of high school, my mother once acknowledged the role the shooting played in our lives, *"How do you protect your kids, how do you preserve their innocence when they've already witnessed something like that!"* Up until then, I had never mused on the shooting's repercussions for any of us, not even for Billy.

* * * * * *

According to family lore, Billy was the unfortunate recipient of an "addictive personality," inheriting the Irish vulnerability to alcohol. I always considered his long deterioration and early death a hapless fate unto itself, but my therapist assigned more significance to the shooting. He encouraged me to explore it further with Paul, which felt like unbolting the lock on the family mausoleum. Paul was relieved, though, even eager to reflect on this painful chapter. He was convinced that Billy's alcoholism was, in large part, an attempt to slay the demons of survivor guilt that tormented him since the shooting. Billy was never the same after that night, Paul said. I had no real appreciation before then for what Billy had been through. It was only the negative effect his life had on mine that had mattered to me.

Paul was often overlooked in the glare of Billy's many

crises, but he also loved him and had compassion for his struggles. He admired Billy's charisma and how well-liked he was in the neighborhood despite his obvious problems. But I hardly knew this brother, seven years my senior; to me, he was the alcoholic sibling with whom I never felt at ease. Friends envied my "cool" older brothers, but the gulf between reality and illusion was dismaying. By the time I was a teenager, Billy was not so much the dashing oldest brother as he was the dissolute child endlessly mired in troublesome circumstances. I watched my parents' helpless anxiety over his drinking, their repeated trips with him to rehab, and their constant strangled heartache each time he relapsed.

There were several "drunks" in our neighborhood whose wobbly gait and ugly slurred speech frightened me. One was the father of a friend in the apartment house next to ours, who tended bar at the saloon on our corner. Like our family, theirs had five children, and when he weaved down the street on his way home from work in the early evenings, I felt sad for everyone in their home. Billy, too, staggered down our block with a crazy light in his eyes, and whenever I saw him coming, I seethed in anger and ran to avoid him. I was consoled, though, by the fact that Billy was not my father, which made their situation seem far worse than mine, but I imagined the sight of both our careening family members provoked the same gut-wrenching feeling.

There was a shady spot at the end of our street where a stray "bum" sometimes lay sleeping. I always approached the area with trepidation and averted my gaze for fear the slumped-over figure propped against the apartment building might one day be Billy. While I lay in bed at night, I listened with a pounding heart for the rhythm of his footsteps in the hallway, trying to determine his degree of inebriation. When he was sufficiently intoxicated, he sometimes cooked for himself in the middle of the night in our tiny kitchen, and the sizzle and smell of that food disgusted me. There were other times when I picked a fight with him, angry at the strife he caused in our home, and we would shout in each other's faces, nose to nose. But mostly, I felt timid around him and tried to stay as far away from him as I could. My mother said he was a "mean drunk," and the times he argued with my father late in the night are among my worst memories. My father would curse then, which he rarely did, and sound bitter, the weariness and despair heavy in his voice. I felt forlorn during those moments and respectful of the grown-up, painful matters he dealt with. In the last years of his life, Billy also succumbed to hard drugs, and he died two months before my mother, at the age of forty-one, homeless, during a late-winter blizzard, in the same park where the fight had started all those years ago.

My father never got over Billy's death and never forgave himself for refusing to take him back into the house shortly before he died. It was the only time he had sent him away when he was in such desperate shape, but with my mother so ill, he had no choice. "Tough love" had not been a concept my parents could fully embrace. He was their first-born pride and joy, and, although they tried, they could not stop seeing that little boy whom they could never abandon. Early on, they tried to keep a tight rein on Billy, but he was incorrigible. He played hooky from high school more than he attended, and the truant officer was often at our door. My parents would drive him to school to ensure his arrival, and he would exit right out the back door before the first period began. Each time I retrieved the mail and found another postcard, "*William has been absent fifty-one days in the past three months,*" I got nervous and hated to hand it over to my mother. Eventually, he dropped out of high school and worked odd jobs for the rest of his life. The first time he disappeared from home, for three straight days, my parents were frantic until my father found him ravaged somewhere after a drunken bender. When he finally brought him home, I understood how a child could break a parent's heart almost beyond repair.

On one of her last lucid days, my brothers and I sat around my mother in her living room while she rocked in her chair, trying to reconcile herself to death, expressing her love and wishes for us. Billy listened from the next room for a few minutes and then burst in, hugged her, fell at her knees, and sobbed in her lap like a child. They were so inextricably bound in their suffering it was hard to watch. She told him merely, impossibly, to "be good" after she was gone.

* * * * * *

It may be there was no correlation between the unprocessed impact of the shooting on my future psychological state; however, years later, when Jimmy and I both developed symptoms of OCD, most of the obsessive thoughts we had focused on guilt of one sort or another. When Jimmy was in high school, for instance, my mother discovered scores of folded-up newspaper clippings under his mattress, all of them accounts of felonies that had occurred throughout Brooklyn. While my mother was perplexed and had no idea what to make of them, I knew that he must be tormenting himself by imagining he had committed those crimes himself.

Unfortunately, I knew what it was to suspect yourself guilty of an unspeakable crime, actions so heinous and foreign to your personality that you drove yourself mad. I offer one piteous example of my own here and will let it suffice for the rest, for these scenarios are too sad and painful to dwell on. It was New Year's Eve of my junior year in high school, and a friend had asked me to take her babysitting job because she had a party to attend. I agreed to help her because I needed the money and had nothing better to do, but I had never babysat before and was uneasy about the responsibility. The infant and toddler slept soundly that evening. I only peeked in on them once or twice, but I worried throughout those hours that I might somehow harm them, especially the infant. I agonized for weeks after that night, worried that something had happened to either of the children while I was there, and I waited anxiously for my friend to casually mention the family so I could be reassured they were all still alive and well. I knew how preposterous it was to think I had hurt those children, but I could not get the thought out of my mind. I was no match for the tenacity of those obsessions, and I hated the fact that while the rest of the world went blithely about their business, I suffered over morose fantasies and the shame of my screwed-up nature.

Chapter 7

I was aware that nothing I told my therapist was so terrible, that multitudes of others had gracefully withstood fates far worse than my own. I was loved and had good parents, and I was not the victim of sexual, physical, or emotional abuse; like most families, we had our share of crises, but it seemed there was no obvious post-traumatic stress to contend with. I could not understand why my reactions to things were so unusual, and I could only conclude there was something grossly wrong with *me*. Thus, I came to believe that the aberrant state of mind I now inhabited was the product of my overly intro-verted nature. *"Were you always shy?"* my therapist asked. *"Yes,"* I said, *"I must have been born that way."* It seemed that I always had steeper social mountains to climb than my more outgoing companions. Interactions they took in stride filled me with fear. I was also extremely sensitive to criticism.

I described to my therapist how on my first day of

kindergarten, an event I looked forward to for weeks, I received what I experienced as a blistering reproach, though in retrospect, I think almost every other five-year-old would have easily sloughed it off in the moment. The teacher called each child's name to come forward and select a plaything from the toy chest. I was happy when she announced my name and began marching to the front of the room when she abruptly shouted, *"Not you—the other Patricia!"* I was so hurt and humiliated by her rude manner that I went home, cried to my mother, and never returned for a second day. I thought my mother was kind not to force me back, but my therapist questioned her wisdom. *Did she not speak up for you and help you work through this? Didn't you ever have someone to help you handle difficult situations? A coach? A mentor? A friend? No*, I answered, again ashamed of my timorous nature.

Over the years, I occasionally attempted to overcome what felt like my huge moral failing by willing myself through excruciating exercises, like an adult education class called "Public Speaking for the Extremely Shy Person." However, any headway I made never stuck. My early unmanaged shyness led to extreme shyness, which led to social anxiety, which led to global social anxiety, which sometimes led to panic attacks, all of which destroyed my confidence and affected my mental health. At one point, I adopted the Alcoholics Anonymous philosophy to help deal with the powerlessness I felt to manage it. I was amazed that a common trait like shyness could so impair me that I was as desperate as all the other overcome souls who reached out to that program. Yet I worked those twelve steps in the hopes that I could make peace with it, and indeed that surrendering had brought a small amount of spiritual consolation to my struggles.

Although examining the roots of my shyness helped me better understand myself, it also compounded my feelings of guilt. I was convinced that I had failed to learn something essential I needed to develop into a normal, functioning human being. The younger version of myself, the one dredged up in therapy, tormented me. I could not stand to reflect upon what my family's experience of me had been. I felt profoundly ashamed of the child I once was—completely shut down, ridiculously oversensitive, peevish to the extreme. *"Why was I like that? Why wasn't I stronger back then? None of my brothers turned out like that. Why was I the only one? There must be something wrong with me!"* I moaned to my therapist. *"It was not your fault,"* he said.

* * * * * *

I had come to therapy the night of that particular exchange drenched in sadness, and as I rambled on drearily to my therapist, the tears flowing, he suddenly said, *"It's time to do an EMDR."* He mentioned EMDRs in the past, but I had no idea what they were, and when I asked him when one might occur, he said only that I was "not ready yet." Now he quickly set up a metal tripod in front of me and plucked a long metal object out of a canvas bag. He set the object on top of the tripod and explained that the EMDR treatment—Eye Movement Desensitization and Reprocessing—would help drain off some of my sadness. I was skeptical of any contrived therapeutic techniques. I felt I was not a good candidate because I had no creative imagination, was not the type to role play, disliked meditation, affirmations, and other self-improvement strategies. On the other hand, I was in agony and was relieved that, at least for a few minutes, someone else would shoulder my burden.

He instructed me to follow a gliding strip of tiny green lights with my eyes as they traversed back and forth along the horizontal metal bar. My job was to notice the sensations which arose in my body as I thought about the topics he brought up. He would monitor my responses, and if the process became too intense, he said he would slow it down. When the going got rough, I was advised to visualize myself in a "safe place," my wraparound front porch on a balmy summer day, for instance. And then he began soothingly narrating his rendition of my personal story. I sat in steely silence, smug in my prediction of failure. *"I don't feel anything,"* I declared; *"this is not going to work!"* He was unfazed and said he had expected as much, knowing how adroitly I blocked emotions. And with that, my efforts to stonewall felt silly. He had seen this all before; I was not so unusual. What was the benefit of my resistance, anyway? *"Wouldn't you rather do this than fade away in the back ward of some hospital?"* he asked. His point hit home. What would I do if therapy did not work? What was the harm of letting go for a change, of following his lead, allowing the emotions to surface, listening to my body? Something gave way within me, and I agreed to try again. We resumed, and almost instantly, I was crying and then sobbing with paroxysms of grief.

He worked in sequences, targeting clusters of memories. While I tracked the sliding green lights, I held those recollections in mind and dissolved into the mental replay, trying not to judge the scenes before me. He explained that if we obstruct emotions for too long, they burrow deep in our minds, creating fissures of pent-up pressure. Under the perfect storm of stress, the fissures tear apart and wreak havoc. *"No wonder you suffered the way you did,"* he said. *"It makes perfect sense that you developed the problems you had."* He reconstructed a different, more positive narrative for me, one I would never have conceived of myself, and then concluded the EMDR with a guided visualization and deep breathing. I was slightly dazed when I left the session, the bloodletting having left me lightheaded. During the ensuing week, I noticed a gradual lightening of spirit, and by the next session, I felt pleasantly distanced from the issues we had confronted during the EMDR.

I consented to several more EMDRs during that year, but none was as powerful as the first. The showers of equanimity were briefer, and the long-term benefits of the reprocessing technique were too far out of reach. I still could not shake my low mood, kept waiting for the other shoe to drop with every step forward. I dreaded my weekly therapy sessions and had to combat the urge to turn the car around each time I set out for my therapist's office. I felt I was too sick for this world, too paranoid, and could see no way out. And then, finally, on a sweltering mid-July afternoon, as the skies cracked open in a roaring thunderstorm, I broke down to my husband and confessed that I was wasted by my encounter with the ghost. I told him I "could not take it anymore," that I could no longer fight or even hang on. I was defeated and, with great anguish, asked if he could possibly call someone, *right this minute*, to help me, to prescribe some medication that might release me from this agony. *Of course, I will, right away,* he said. He immediately called our family physician, and within a few hours, I swallowed my first dose of medication and prayed for blessed relief.

* * * * * *

For the first few days on medication, there were mild side effects of nausea and drowsiness, but after that, I could almost pinpoint the moment when my surging anxiety short-circuited, bypassing its usual stormy course through my body. I worried it was too good to be true, a false harbinger of hope. In time, though, the worst of my paranoia waned—the trees looked like trees again—and very, very gradually, the dark veil lifted. As the weeks passed, I felt incrementally more energized, less ashamed, and more willing to look at Annie's problems objectively rather than as my ghostly projection. I was eating, sleeping, and exercising again, sometimes even venturing to look people in the eye without dread. One afternoon while walking with my dog, dabs of softly hued flowers in a neighbor's garden caught my attention, and I thought what a long time it had been since I had noticed *anything* bright or cheery. It struck such a pure chord of beauty in my soul, I can still recall that simple moment of joy today.

My therapist said he noticed subtle shifts in my demeanor, less lachrymose maunderings, some decisive talk of the future, and occasional sparks of humor. I came clean with him about my new regimen of medication without referencing the suicidal agony that preceded it. He never knew how lethally stalled the therapeutic process had become for me. No one, not even my husband, needed to know those dismal details. Instead, I recommitted to working through my issues, and we continued together for several more months. As that year came full circle and the next chilling February arrived, I felt ready to act on my own and leave behind the intense introspection of the therapy room.

I could see now that there was some logic to my life's trajectory and that my responses to overwhelming struggles were uniquely human. I knew that my complexities and weaknesses issued from a myriad of unavoidable influences and were not indelible defects in my character that needed to be shrouded in secrecy. I also knew that I could potentially inhabit any of the phantasms dormant in my mind, but that *I was not them* and these same capacities existed in everyone. The darker and more despairing aspects of human nature were now more fully illuminated, and I felt far less desire to hide these "unacceptable" sides of myself.

If I had participated more fully in the therapeutic process and revealed every last paranoid or depressive thought, my therapist might have reassured me more, or sooner, but my diffident, reserved nature and the severity of my symptoms prohibited such disclosures. On the other hand, had I been medicated sooner, had the ghost and I not crossed over that threshold of sanity into madness, I might never have understood its purpose in my life or truly laid it to rest.

Medication helped treat my most debilitating symptoms and jump-started the healing process that had begun months earlier with the honest hashing out of issues, stories, and history in an open and supportive dialogue. If there was a placebo effect attached to that medication, it lay in the possibility of hope; while those pills may have worked out bugs in my brain and adjusted or enhanced neurological deficits, they also intimated a strength and confidence I did not truly have.

As I slowly steadied myself post-therapy, my concerns swung back to my daughter. There was work to be done, and she needed me.

Chapter 8

> "Confined in the dark, narrow cage of our own
> making which we take for the whole universe,
> very few of us can even begin to imagine another
> dimension of reality."
>
> *The Tibetan Book of Living and Dying, Sogyal Rinpoche*

Mike and I redoubled our efforts to help Annie, which first meant closing the door on any religious instruction and facilitating her transition to the public school. When she walked out the front doors of that Catholic school for the last time on a humid June morning, we breathed a sigh of relief that her season in hell was finally over. Our mission now was to exhume the old Annie, the pre-second grade Annie. Sister Maria was sent away "on retreat," and, as far as we know, never returned to our area. The school shut down completely a few years later, but it still stands, desolate, with its broken colored panes of glass in the gymnasium windows and a rusty "For Sale" sign still staked in the sparse grass.

We essentially deserted the Catholic Church after that, which was not all that unusual at the time. Stories of abuse were rampant in the media and within our own communities. I knew there were plenty of good parishioners and clergy in the Church, but neither Mike nor I could ignore the damage done to our daughter for the greater good of Catholicism. Yet there was still a loyal, nostalgic part of me that felt a sense of responsibility to the Catholic tradition. I had not hailed from a particularly religious background, but my brothers and I all went to Catholic grammar school and were brought up to attend Sunday mass. To completely forsake this heritage felt like severing the last ties with home, abolishing any trace of religious support. Beyond rescuing Annie from a harmful environment, I needed to know more about what I was renouncing, and when I recovered enough from my own emotional crisis to continue my graduate school studies, I dedicated myself to an education in the great Catholic theologians and philosophers.

Before Annie's misfortune, it seemed right that my children had at least some religious foundation for moral guidance and spiritual comfort or, perhaps later, to provide them a vantage point for further exploration. I had a certain fondness, too, for the Catholic nuns and could recall a couple of exceedingly kind ones from my own school days. I was predisposed to like and esteem Sister Maria, which I did at first, but the events of that year destroyed any inclination I had to look past her behavior and remain within the Catholic fold. By the conclusion of my limited, though rigorous research over several years at Villanova University, I was satisfied that in our family's situation, the elimination of a Catholic inculcation for Annie was appropriate and necessary. If she were to seek a spiritual outlet or community in the future, it would be by her own choice and on her own terms.

The trials with Sister Maria had brought complex spiritual issues to the forefront for me. Even Annie's first communion, despite the colossal underlying conflict, held moments of awe.

I had slogged through the preparations for that day with disgust, impatient to get the ceremony over with and move Annie out of that school. I purchased the white communion dress, veil, and shoes perfunctorily, with rancor, even. On the appointed morning, Mike and I stood in Annie's classroom amid the gaggle of excited children and watched while the other parents snapped class pictures with a sweetly smiling Sister Maria. My stomach roiled with the knowledge that only a week prior, Annie had finally been granted formal "approval" to receive communion with the rest of the class. An hour later, though, when those second graders proceeded in pairs down the long nave of the softly lit church, amid the strains of a quietly beautiful hymn I had never heard before, their hands pressed together in front of them like cherubs, a hush descended upon the proceedings and tears flowed down my face.

During my studies at Villanova, I took special care to examine the genesis of the Catholic belief in "original sin," the supposed ancestral stain on our souls we are born with as a result of Eve's disobedience in the Garden of Eden. I came away disillusioned with this doctrine and felt it was time for me to stand by my own convictions. If evil and sin existed in this world, I did not believe it was as a preexisting condition to be ferreted out in innocent children. I subscribed more to another line of thought: "We enter a broken and torn and sinful world—that is for sure. But we do not enter as blotches on existence, as sinful creatures; we burst into the world as 'original blessings'" (Fox).

* * * * * *

Religion was a complicated subject I had been turning over in my mind since my early twenties when I had an accidental life-changing spiritual experience. To write of such things risks sounding daft, eccentric, or grandiose, but it was the cornerstone of my formation as a more mature human being and the reason I progressed in life despite my untreated mental health problems. It also helps clarify why I found the clash with Sister Maria so disturbing and her actions so vile.

I was twenty-one years old at the time, commuting to college and working as a part-time secretary in Manhattan. At home, tensions were high as Billy was hospitalized and on the verge of death from alcoholism, though he later survived this crisis. I was also in the midst of a difficult romantic relationship that had left me shaken to the core. On a wintry afternoon, as I scurried through the streets on some neighborhood chores, lost in thought, I very uncharacteristically stepped inside our parish church. I was the only person present in the hundreds of pews around me, and as I sat there, immersed in the stillness, I prayed, simply and sincerely, for "peace of mind," nothing more.

My personal circumstances did not change after that, but a few weeks later, as I sat at my desk at home trying to finish a term paper, my concentration badly frayed, I suddenly and categorically announced out loud, "*I give up,*" conceding to my helplessness and consciously letting go of the thing I had been striving for, the reciprocal devotion of this first-time love. My mind went completely blank for a few seconds, and then, in the next instant, I was seized by the perception that our human existence was meaningless, that our actions amounted to nothing in the grand scheme of things, and that there was no higher purpose to life or to our suffering. I was completely deflated. After another pregnant pause, an impulse burst from within me. An unexpected "decision" sprang from my lips, urging me to keep moving along the path I was on, to keep loving this person—because *I want to!* Prior to this, I did not see any decision to be made. The surprise "choice" felt wondrously liberating, as if it had spontaneously "popped" out of me, releasing a joyous, deep-seated sensation of well-being. In the glow of this euphoria, the previous distress I felt over my personal circumstances evaporated, burning off like the morning mist beneath a radiant noonday sun.

The next day, standing on the subway platform on my way to work, I was overwhelmed by a supreme feeling of happiness; this surprising joy so enlivened me that I felt ready to die, right there on the platform, as if I had achieved the ultimate satisfaction in life, the natural conclusion after which there was nothing further to do or experience. But then, over the next two or three days, a series of events, or moments, occurred, too intimate to articulate here, which ushered in radical transformations of feeling and shifting realities, all of it unfolding and evolving until a profound new harmony of awareness occurred. During the experience, I had never felt saner, clearer, or more certain of myself. I felt so exhilaratingly wide awake that I could barely sleep. The only way to accurately describe these days was as a type of enlightenment experience, the culmination of which was an expansion of consciousness and an ecstasy of rapturous emotion; it was as if I were one with the blissful heart of the universe.

I was bedazzled when it was all over. The unintentional "choice" I made while sitting at my desk days before was somehow the impetus to this mysterious flow of events, the turning point after which I found myself in something of an alternate world. It was only later, through serendipitous reading and carefully chosen college courses—"psychology and religion," for instance—that I came to recognize and name what happened to me. Commonly known as "mystical" experiences, these occurrences are transitory lapses of time in which the boundaries between one's personal consciousness and the fundamental life force of the cosmos—"the hidden, invisible, yet pulsing, breathing, singing source of it all"—merge together in an all-encompassing, unified whole (Moore).

The schema I most closely identified with in my studies at that time was Carl Jung's process of "individuation." As a final project one semester, I analyzed the stages of the experience within his framework. Jung theorized that at various, usually troubling times in our lives, the God-archetype, or the sacred ground of the human psyche, abruptly manifests into consciousness and eventually, if all goes well, fuses with the ego, the nucleus of our personality, to form a new, more comprehensive whole. Since my experience involved a spiritual merging with a divine *other*, the "numinous," it could also be interpreted within any theological ideology as a serious religious experience of overpowering love and ineffable beauty.

In practical terms, the net result of the experience was a great settling within me, a new openness and thirst for knowledge, and an awareness of the hallowed essence of our human nature. I understood this divinity as both innate *and* external to me; I *knew* there was a force greater than any individual consciousness in the world, an infinite source of love I could honor and draw comfort from. During the experience, there was a consummate lack of fear and an intense, though impersonal, feeling of love for every person with whom I came in contact. The world existed in a state of exquisite perfection, and everything made complete sense. In the final stage of the process, there came a dramatic humbling, a sudden cessation of the state of ecstasy, a moment when I grasped our human limitations. It was the moment when I came back "down to earth," so to speak, and realized that those limitations were what made us human, were part and parcel of the whole. As that grounding humility rushed through me, I was compelled to write down insights that came to me, which turned out to be a catalog of my shortcomings, simple phrases about my weaknesses, and how they were all "*okay.*" A gust of cosmic humor swept through me, and my final insight was a reminder not to take myself too seriously.

The overall "lesson" I gleaned was to live life as much as possible in the present, as if each day were my last, a timeworn aphorism, to be sure, but one that spoke directly to my anxious soul.

As I once again turned my attention to the everyday concerns of life, I felt peaceful, serene, my enduring agitation having washed away in that sea of bliss. I no longer felt the need to struggle as I had before, for the desires and attachments that plagued me faded from my life as if I had inexplicably transcended them. The urgency of that first love dissipated as though all along it had been a stepping-stone to this greater love. The mystical experience shined a light on the unique beauty of each human being, and I knew that the unifying bond of love was what upheld the universe; in fact, it seemed that love was the very essence of the universe.

All of this knowledge had a salutary effect on me. I was more self-assured and independent, yet still the same person I had always been, with the same emotional makeup and vulnerabilities. That transporting mystical experience did not guarantee a lasting beatific happiness, nor did it obviate future personal crises, yet I have remained faithful to its truth and clarity of vision, even though I could not always live according to its wisdom.

My attitude toward religion was, therefore, unorthodox. Over the years, I discovered parallels to this experience in religions and cultures around the globe and had grown confident in both its value and validity. However, I seldom indulged my spiritual leanings beyond the many books I read. But now, as I resumed my life post-therapy, I found that one of the many gifts of therapy I received was the ability to prize my spiritual side once again.

When I returned to graduate school after my emotional breakdown, I was fortunate to have a mentor who encouraged my study in the philosophy of religion. This forced me to apply cool logic to the exalted passion of a religious experience. I came to admire the seriousness of Catholicism, its appreciation of human suffering, and its comfort with mystery. I no longer held literally to the tenets of its doctrines, but I agreed with many of its ethical teachings and its emphasis on social justice. The human nature I encountered during that mystical union was replete with goodness, so when my daughter began to worry about her sinful nature, the Devil, and the fires of Hell more than she could take in any message of God's love, religion became a real-life crucible rather than a mostly benign system of faith and worship.

Chapter 9

"… there were moments with my daughter when I
had the distressed sense of being in the presence of
a rare force of nature, such as a great blizzard
or flood: destructive, but in its way astounding too."

Hurry Down Sunshine, Michael Greenberg

We first attempted therapy for Annie while she was still in second grade, in the belly of the beast. When she came home from school one day that spring, laden with her usual anxiety, I hoisted her onto my lap and suggested we might visit someone, a psychologist perhaps, to talk about the diffi-culties she was having. In that moment, I could see the fear in her eyes that her experience of the world was not quite right and that she might be somehow different from other people. She cried softly into my shoulder and asked, *"Does that mean there's something wrong with me?"* *"No, no,"* I quickly re-assured her, *"it would just be nice to talk with someone who might be able to help you with your worries."*

I took her for a few sessions with my own therapist, who was already well-versed in her story, but I was naively opti-mistic, imagining a quick, dramatic cure. It started out well enough as he commiserated with her troubles. He tried to establish a rapport with her through play—hiding candy around his office, allowing his pets to strut in one at a time, kicking the soccer ball around with her in his yard—but when he tried to guide her through an EMDR, all therapy crashed and burned. The process was too intense and scary for her. We quickly let therapy drop, but to this day, she winces when she remembers how those gliding green lights felt like the devil's eyes boring into her soul.

At home, Mike and I tended to act as if the emotional abuse from second grade had been a bad dream. We erased all religious terminology from our vocabularies and gave churches a wide berth. As the distance between Sister Maria and us grew, we tried to brighten the atmosphere in our home by joking more, singing and dancing more, and taking any opportunity to "lighten up." We poked fun at ourselves, attempting to demonstrate how imperfect we all were as human beings. We encouraged Annie to express herself through art, dance, fashion, sports, all the outlets she already enjoyed, and then some. By August, when she got frustrated with an art project, she turned to me and said, *"Oh, well, nobody's perfect."* One day we realized she was laughing again, not often, but in a lighthearted manner we had not heard in almost a year.

In September, she started third grade at the public elementary school, and I briefed her new teacher on the events of the previous year at our first parent-teacher conference. She was so clearly sympathetic to Annie's suffering that it brought tears to my eyes. Annie quickly took a liking to her and said she was *"nothing like Sister Maria."* Within a few months, some of Annie's OCD symptoms, like counting, dropped off, but she was still anxious and preoccupied and brushed her fingerprints off every surface she touched. In time she regained some of her feistiness and made several new friends. These early signs of recovery buoyed us and gave us tentative hope that the worst was behind us.

When she was in third grade, we had her evaluated by a kind female psychiatrist who determined that while Annie's symptoms at that time did not require medication, she could benefit from "cognitive behavioral therapy" (CBT) to help deal with her OCD. Commonly used to treat psychological disorders like anxiety, depression, and phobias, CBT takes a relatively short-term approach to mental distress as opposed to psychotherapy's meandering search for unconscious conflicts. Cognitive behavioral therapy aims to teach patients that while they cannot control troubling events in their lives, they can control how they deal with them in the present. Patients work toward incremental change by practicing new coping skills, first in therapy and then out in the world. For Annie, the goal was to grapple with her irrational fears by learning to recognize and actively challenge the underlying thoughts which gave rise to them.

She was assigned a gentle, young female psychologist named Laura, who tried to help Annie understand the extreme unlikeliness that any of her OCD worries would come to pass. Annie enjoyed chatting with Laura and drawing pictures for her, such as a parachute with trailing cords attached, each carrying another of her OCD fears. She confided in Laura as best she could, but she was often bored and impatient for the session to end. Considering her young age and the stress she had already endured, we encouraged Annie to stay in therapy but did not insist. She also participated in a support group with other struggling pre-adolescent girls, but it disbanded after six months, and we were unable to find another one.

By fourth grade, Annie demonstrated above-average proficiency in literature and writing, as well as a decided deficiency in math. Fifth grade revealed further academic struggles and the early onset of puberty, but by elementary school gradua-tion, she had matured into an intelligent, artistic, and occa-sionally very funny—"hysterical," I often called her—individ-ual, with emotional depth and physical beauty. We used to say that if she could learn to channel her creative energies, she had greatness in her. Thrilled at the apparent turnaround of so much psychological damage, we marveled at what we per-ceived as her poignant rebirth.

However, by fifth grade, she was also tired of any kind of therapy and refused to continue with her sessions.

＊ ＊ ＊ ＊ ＊ ＊

Annie started middle school with a bang. Upon arriving home each day, when I greeted her with the usual, *"How do you like it so far? How are your teachers? What are your classmates like?"* she invariably responded, *"Fabulous! It's great! I love it!"* But when I asked for more details, she was close-mouthed and grew more irritable by the day. There were new signs of anxiety, of fighting to keep things under tight control. Every-thing had to be balanced and symmetrical, like how many times she brushed her teeth on each side and where exactly she situated herself on the couch—right in the middle, to allow equal space on both sides. She avoided taking showers because she felt the bathtub drain had taken on some malevolent quality, and consequently, personal hygiene was another new challenge. She was aloof and surly and detached herself more and more from the sisters next door.

Halfway through the school year, Annie came to us in tears one night and revealed that she was being bullied at school. She begged us not to get involved, claiming it would only make matters worse. We coached her on how to stand up for herself, encouraged her to report the harassment to the school administrators, and urged her to seek help from the guidance counselors. I read up on the "culture of girls," in which "queen bees" ruled and girls treated each other badly, but there was also bullying from boys, which blindsided her. They mocked her march-to-my-own-drummer style and treated her with brutal insensitivity when rumors of her mental health problems began circulating. On the sly, I called one of the boys I suspected had a hand in the slandering, but he wriggled off the hook, pleading total innocence.

Academically, she lost all interest, barely passing most classes. Her irritability soon turned combative and then explosive. She was more secretive and attached to her cell phone, and some light surveillance of her texting uncovered several sexually provocative messages. When we confronted her, she sat at our kitchen table so deadpan and defiant that a shiver ran through me. I kept asking her why she did this, what motivated her, but she only blinked her eyes slowly and gazed off into space. "*Why?*" I kept repeating until finally, she grudgingly responded, in tears, "*I'm not good enough! I'm just not good enough ... in any way!*" We reminded her how beautiful and talented she was and how much people liked her, but it did nothing to lessen her despair. She was too sad to listen, and, besides, we were her parents, not her peers. Our opinion meant little.

That pained admission was a glimpse into Annie's innermost being. It had only been four years since she was so frightened and consumed with guilt she could hardly breathe. The association between these two periods in her life was hazy, the incidents of second grade too dissimilar to the current blows; however, when she cried, "I'm not good enough!" the anguish in her voice seemed to come from the same dark place.

* * * * * *

Things got worse after that. She retreated from one friend

after another, sure that everyone hated her. At home, she became enraged if you so much as looked at her the wrong way, and she would fight you to the death over trivialities, absurdities. She vandalized her room by defacing the walls and carved hateful messages on her bed frame, closet door, and dresser. There were times she was physically aggressive, striking walls, doors, and anything in her path, hollering and looming over us so threateningly that, short of pummeling her, there was no way out of this horrifying situation but to call the police. Even their imposing presence did not completely tame her, but she checked herself enough to desist from attacking. And then, when she was still in seventh grade, I picked up the phone one night and overheard her agreeing to pick up drugs from a classmate at school, after which she completely denied the conversation.

We tried our best to restrain her, but the methods of discipline we used with our son had no effect on her. We established reasonable, clear rules and communicated our expectations; we discussed the issues, expressed our loving concern, and listened to her feedback; we leveraged privileges, withheld electronics, and other possessions; we sought guidance from family, friends, and experts, and through it all she fought back like a wild stallion. Punishments and consequences backfired in a fusillade of fury. She refused to be corralled and spent most of her time at home arguing and yelling at me at the top of her lungs. As she shrieked, I ran around the house closing windows, attempting in vain to keep the neighbors out of our business, and no sooner did I open them again than it was time to dash back around and close them.

Somehow, we managed to coerce her back into therapy and obtain another psychiatric evaluation. Bipolar disorder was the first major diagnosis to come down the pike, and though the difficult and chronic nature of this illness was disheartening, I cried with relief when I heard it because at least it provided some rationale for the chaos we were living through. The psychiatrist also gave us hope that with proper medication and effective treatment, Annie's rage could be tempered, and she might find some peace. Though the classic mood swings and other compulsive behaviors typically associated with the bipolar label did not accurately capture Annie's condition, there were enough nuances to the disorder that we trusted the diagnosis and braced ourselves for what lay ahead. I also discovered there was a less familiar sub-type of bipolar disorder, which was characterized primarily by irritability, which had been Annie's defining characteristic almost since birth.

Chapter 10

"It is in your own best interest not to respond to
borderline rage with rage of your own."

Stop Walking on Eggshells, Paul T. Mason, M.S., Randi Kreger

Annie complied with the regimen of medication for bipolar disorder and weekly therapy for months, with no improvement. At the same time, I kept finding open safety pins lying around and eventually realized there was no coincidence between the scabs and scratches I noticed on her limbs and those sharp objects. "Cutting" had become her primary coping mechanism. It was hard to grasp how the superficial slashes on her wrists, thighs, and abdomen could be an outlet for emotional pain and how a self-imposed physical injury might cancel out inner torment, but, as we learned, this external release can neutralize psychological suffering and divert attention away from the real wound, the invisible psychological one. The cutter also controls how, when, and what degree of damage to inflict, which bestows a small amount of mastery over the pain. And not least of its merits, cutting can be a form of self-punishment, something Annie may have unconsciously felt she deserved since second grade.

There were apparently many triggers for Annie's cutting, but the one I knew best was the constant arguments we had at home. Though she mostly kept these gashes hidden from us, there was the occasional intentional exhibition of some fresh laceration to demonstrate, however manipulatively, the deep dimensions of her misery. The alarm Mike and I felt when we caught sight of these lesions was difficult to conceal, but they were not life-threatening, and we had to practice neither overreacting nor underreacting to this self-harming behavior.

One night in early seventh grade, she swallowed a fistful of antianxiety medication in a halfhearted suicide attempt. Before I went to bed, she wished me goodnight and told me she loved me, and then soon after I fell asleep, she woke me in a panic to tell me what she had done and beg for help. This led to her first hospitalization, at which point another psychiatrist diagnosed emerging "borderline personality disorder" (BPD), a pronouncement most psychiatrists are reluctant to make in adolescents for fear of labeling them with one of the most stigmatizing and intractable of all disorders, even before their personalities fully develop.

BPD was a relatively new and notoriously hard-to-pin-down diagnosis, even among professionals. It overlaps and mimics the symptoms of other personality and mental disorders and can be either a secondary diagnosis or contribute to the development of other primary ones. The pessimism intrinsic to the BPD label lies in the bundle of problematic features at its core. Unlike the more transient psychological difficulties weathered by most adolescents, individuals with BPD experience chronic distress and almost no sustained periods of contentment. The characteristics of BPD are deeply ingrained, do not respond well to medication, and are amenable to change only very gradually through prolonged therapy over the course of years.

The hallmarks of BPD are fear of abandonment and rejection, hypersensitivity to criticism, persistent feelings of emptiness, frequent and inappropriate displays of anger and rage, self-injurious behavior, fragile and confused sense of identity, idealization and demonization of others (black-and-white thinking), self-destructive tendencies, suicidal thoughts, difficulty regulating emotions, and impulsivity. The clinical picture of BPD more closely approximated Annie's condition, but the primary diagnosis of bipolar disorder was still on the table. As Dr. Blaise Aguirre writes in his book, *Borderline Personality Disorder in Adolescents,* "There is something particularly elusive about borderline personality disorder, especially in adolescents. It seems to overlap with many of the behaviors of normal adolescence and also with post-traumatic stress disorder (PTSD), bipolar disorder, and attention deficit disorder (ADD). BPD is all of those conditions at once and then none at all. Sitting with adolescents with BPD is unlike sitting with any other group. It is as distinct as being with someone with autism or Down Syndrome, but trying to capture what makes it so is difficult at best. Adolescents with BPD don't have the social deficits of autism, the disheveled appearance of depression, the disorganized thinking of psychosis, the grandiosity of mania, or the cravings of addiction. Yet frequently, the scars on their arms bear testament to lives of misery and inner pain."

Researchers attribute both hereditary and environmental factors to the onset of BPD, with a heavy emphasis on various forms of abuse, most commonly sexual, as well as early parental negligence or abandonment. We objected to that innuendo, but we also had to admit there was the neglect of parents who failed to quickly remove Annie from a toxic school environment, the emotional abuse by Sister Maria, the psychic shock of bullying, the fear and confusion around the rising tensions within our home, and the muddle of some degree of drug use, just to name a few of the factors we knew about, not to mention the risk posed by her own psychological vulnerability. As her first psychiatrist in third grade told her, not unkindly, *"You just have an anxious brain. Some children do and some don't. You do."*

In *I Hate You, Don't Leave Me,* Jerold Kreisman writes, "The question of which is the chicken and which is the egg may be impossible to resolve, but the development of illnesses associated with BPD may represent a kind of psychological vulnerability to stress. Just as certain individuals may have genetic and biological vulnerabilities to physical diseases—heart attacks, cancers, gastrointestinal disorders, etc.—many may also have biologically determined propensities to psychiatric illnesses, particularly when stress is added."

Fortunately, there was new optimism regarding the treatment of BPD. With medication to alleviate the more acute symptoms of anxiety and depression, and effective long-term psychotherapy, real progress was believed attainable. Dialectical behavioral therapy (DBT) was the current gold-standard treatment for borderline personality disorder, a process that pits the difficult-to-handle patient against the unconditionally supportive therapist in a quest for positive change or resolution. The goal of dialectical-behavioral therapy is for individuals to learn to accept and tolerate their powerful emotions without judgment and without resorting to self-destructive behaviors. The burden falls heavily upon the therapist to provide unequivocal acceptance and validation of the patient's feelings while at the same time teaching them healthier ways to manage and regulate those emotions, something Mike and I, as Annie's battle-weary parents, were completely unable to do.

After Annie's first hospitalization, her former therapist agreed to take her back as a patient. We also found a DBT support group for adolescent and teenage girls; however, most members of the group were a few years older than Annie and further down the self-destructive path. We soon realized the danger of this dynamic, as Annie was more intrigued by these girls and their flagrant behaviors than wary of them. Individuals with BPD are said to be like empty vessels, impressionable and susceptible to molding themselves around the identity of others they admire (the "chameleon effect") as they struggle to fit in. In addition to this hazard, Annie disliked the group's facilitator and was not engaged in the assigned exercises or homework. The potential for harm, therefore, was greater than for good, and we stopped taking her.

The chameleon effect was a constant threat during her subsequent hospitalizations. One particularly unsettling image stands out of Annie reuniting with one of her old inpatient friends during the "partial" phase of hospitalization when former inpatients try to ease back into the school environment by first participating in a handful of academic classes administered by the hospital. When Annie spotted her friend at the end of the corridor, she raced to embrace her with overwrought excitement. The girl appeared equally giddy to see Annie and was clad in a brief tank top and shorts, with almost every exposed skin surface etched with slashes and scabs. I knew Annie idolized her and envied her artistic talent and panache, but it was not until that moment that I perceived the spooky resemblance between them, right down to the exact same pattern of cuts on their shoulders, arms, and legs.

Journal writing was always a prescribed exercise at the psychiatric hospitals, and Annie's pages from those stays were dense with outpourings of what seemed to me at the time like fantastical embellishments of adolescent angst. Intense relationships sprang up among the inpatients, and she would suddenly find she could not live without the attentions of some fellow patient. I imagined these romantic fantasies were like a balm to her searing loneliness and self-loathing; whichever new idealized companion there was on the unit who flattered her and extended the hope of a future perfect relationship became the embodiment of her reason for being.

While the hospitalizations were always tough—the desperate calls from Annie to get her "out of" there, the heart-wrenching visits with her, the concern over her treatment and anxiety for the future—they were also the only respite we had from unremitting stress. When she came back home, crisis followed upon crisis, and it was impossible to distinguish willful adolescent rebellion from the psychological symptoms of some mental disorder. She continued to strike out and rage on, like a tinderbox ready to explode at the slightest provocation.

The energy Annie expended in public to curb her immense anxiety went haywire at home, and I repeatedly failed in my attempts to disengage from her outbursts. Nothing I said or did made sense to her. *"You don't know what you're talking about!"* she continually screamed at me. Once something set her off, she was incapable of backing down. If I walked away from her tirade, she would become even more enraged. She was louder than I was, deafeningly shrill and vicious, cutting me off mid-sentence with foul language and other vitriol. If I resorted to nastiness, she got nastier. My only recourse in these situations was to shut down emotionally and create a cushion of mental space between us, which she hated. When I told her she was out of line, disrespectful and hostile, that I would not do battle with her and had no choice but to leave the room, she physically blocked my exit—*"Don't you dare walk away from me!"* she shrieked. If I sought refuge in my room, barricaded with a large block of wood across the door, she pounded on it until the panels cracked and split. She broke things, threw things, crushed things in fits of rage. Therapists coached me on ways to hold my ground during these assaults, but it was always easier said than done. She pursued me from room to room to keep the fight alive, refusing to back down. Inevitably, at a certain point, my own temper discharged in a blitz of obscenities until, desperate to get away, I grabbed my car keys and fled the house. An hour or two of driving finally silenced the ringing in my ears and settled me down enough to slink back home, drained and defeated.

It took days, sometimes weeks, for me to recover from these brawls, while Annie bounced back within the hour. Mike had already taken his turn in the ring with her, his temper usually detonating more rapidly and powerfully than my own, but neither of us could go the distance. Our ability to work together as a team to calm her down strained the marriage and underscored our other incompatibilities.

I told him he was a better natural parent and nurturer than I was, yet his stricter disciplinary measures were un-yielding and often ignited her worst rages. My methods, on the other hand, were inconsistent; I was too quick to soften my stance and did too much negotiating. Inadvertently, I placed him in the bad-cop role, leaving him to finish whatever unpleasant business I left hanging. He rightfully resented this, just as I resented his fault-finding with my own measures until I was too self-conscious to reprimand Annie if he was any-where near me. Mike reasoned that if the children feared him, they would more likely respect and obey him, which in turn would lead to less discipline in the first place. I saw the wis-dom in what he said, but I disliked it in practice and recoiled at the words "fear" and "obey." He modeled his father's disciplinary tactics, while I had no good model because I had never been disciplined by either parent. Although I had read the latest child-rearing books and knew the most humane parenting theories, he had the strength to enforce the rules in the real world. He was convinced the old-fashioned methods were best, while I had no use for his know-it-all attitude or authoritarian impulses. He was angry that I seemed not to trust him to remain in control when disciplining, which I denied, while knowing it was somewhat true. I felt at times he could be *too* strict, and I often flew to either child's room to defuse an argument that seemed unnecessarily drawn-out or had escalated to an uncomfortable level. I tried not to get in his way but could not help it, which incensed him. This jousting went on for years until the bitterness on both sides corroded the relationship, and we reached an ugly impasse.

Ideally, we might have blended our parenting styles and derived comfort from moderating and sheltering each other, but our differing approaches were too entrenched and had created an impossible tension. We lost all sense of humor and perspective, both off and on the battlefield. Mike said he would go to his death knowing he had done right by our children, that he was fighting the long war for their character, while I maintained that preserving the relationship with them in the short term was our only hope for success down the road. Where Mike attributed stubborn defiance to Annie's more difficult behaviors, I perceived impaired mental health, but either ratio proved our Waterloo. The marriage suffered, our feelings toward each other deteriorated, and he eventually decided to leave. However upsetting the breakup, I knew we could not survive under the same roof, and though I was heartbroken, I admired his resolve to put an end to our unbearable situation. He was a good man, supportive in innumerable ways, but I hoped Annie would fare better living with just me for a while, without the complication of our conflicting dynamics. The nadir of our family relations occurred several months later when Joe arrived home from a college semester abroad to find his parents separated, his father not living at home, and his sister hospitalized after yet one more appalling crisis.

Chapter 11

"So wherever I am, there's always Pooh,
There's always Pooh and Me.
'What would I do?' I said to Pooh,
'If it wasn't for you,' and Pooh said: 'True,
It isn't much fun for One, but Two
Can stick together,' says Pooh, says he.
'That's how it is,' says Pooh."

"Us Two," A. A. Milne

Around this time, Annie was also experiencing, as she would for years to come, bruising grief over the loss of her one solid companion. The friendship began the summer before Annie started third grade, just as she was regaining some of her old sparkle after that traumatic school year. A new family had moved in across the street, and Annie's curiosity was piqued by one of the two daughters who looked about her age and wore a trendy skull cap with dangling beaded braids. After the family settled in for about a week, Annie headed out the door one afternoon, intent on befriending her. *"I think this is the beginning of a beautiful friendship!"* she quipped before skipping out the door. The girl's name was Cara, and for three years the relationship lived up to that sanguine prediction.

They were prepubescent soulmates, and Annie became an adopted sibling of sorts in Cara's family. The parents married in their teens and were relaxed and adventurous in ways that Mike and I were not. They purchased a motor home on a whim, and Annie traveled throughout the country with them. They took in dogs and cats, had more children, and embraced life with gusto. They seemed to "get" Annie, counteracted her fears and irritability with humor, and Annie found in them a near-perfect substitute family and distraction from her worries.

But as Cara was set to start middle school, the family was lured to sunny California, where they had close relatives, and the temperate weather was more to their liking. They breezed out as swiftly as they breezed in, and Annie was devastated. The following summer, they paid half her airfare and all other expenses so she could spend several weeks with them in their new home. They vacationed in Disneyland, traveled the West Coast, and had their usual freewheeling adventures. The family's newest baby was given the middle name "Annie" to commemorate the special place she held in their hearts. Cara came to stay with us the summer after that, and though we tried to reciprocate with jolly escapades of our own, she missed the bustle of her own family, and her reunion with Annie was not exactly the happy one we anticipated.

Annie clung to Cara's memory throughout the middle school years, dreaming about them almost nightly. When Annie was in seventh grade, Cara's parents demonstrated their affection for Annie in an unusual way. A couple of months prior, I had received a call from Annie's therapist who told me she was legally bound to inform me that Annie was using drugs, some type of pills. Annie exploded in rage when I brought up the phone call and refused to see this therapist, or any other one, again. Another hospitalization followed, and after ten days, she came home with the same defiant attitude.

When Cara's family learned how alarming our situation had become, they invited Annie to go live with them in California, and Annie jumped at the chance.

Cara's mother was sure she could "get through to Annie," and, after much agonizing, Mike and I agreed to this unconventional arrangement. By then, if there was a path that offered Annie even a glimmer of hope for a brighter future, we were willing to pursue it. With the assurance that Cara's parents would seek psychiatric care for Annie, all four parents signed on to the experiment. A flurry of details followed—legal letters, administrative approvals, school transfer documentation. I was despondent and sobbed for days leading up to her departure. I bought her a gold heart locket with the words "I Love You" engraved on it so she would have a tangible reminder of me and channeled my grief into a letter I gave her just before she left:

> *How can I possibly express my sorrow as a mother right now? I see the wisdom in this separation, yet I fear losing the maternal bond that has given my life wonderful meaning. Though I know you the best and love you the most, I realize my influence may not be what you need right now. Your trials have weighed on my mind, your secret agonies have haunted me, and your harsh self-doubts have pained me. You are often such a shattering reflection of my own self as a child and teenager that I have felt terribly responsible for somehow passing on to you my own troubled essence. I wish I had gotten the appropriate help when I was young and had come to terms with my own mental health problems, for I might have been a better role model for you, known the right things to say and do, danced with your nature less rigidly and fearfully. But I vowed years ago to help ease your struggles, whatever the cost, and now I see how dearly I must pay.*

It has been my privilege and joy to care for you and love you, but the turbulent waters of adolescence have carried us to the brink. I took for granted that you would be with me until you were ready to move on as a young adult, and I mourn the chance to witness your next stage of life. How striking this turn of events! I pray that its benefits will outweigh the solid security of living in your own home, however imperfect.

Everything that happens to you matters to me at the deepest level of my being. Even though I will not be with you, I will try my best to lovingly watch over you in spirit. So go now and flourish in California. Fill your life with the good and happy things that have eluded you. Enjoy the young children about you, how they so trustingly look up to you. Seek out friends who will support you and appreciate your strengths as well as your weaknesses. Work steadily toward goals that will satisfy you and strengthen your intimacy with the world. Respect and love Cara's parents, who have magnanimously stepped into this most important role.

Do not forget that my first wish is always for you to live with me, and whenever, or if ever, you decide that the time is right for you to return, I will be elated.

* * * * * *

She was back before the week was out. By the time her plane alighted in San Francisco, Annie said she realized that she had made a terrible mistake. She called and texted me with frantic messages. She soon found she was not able to slip into the surrogate family as seamlessly as she had imagined. According to Annie, Cara's mother became suddenly brusque and hard-nosed about restrictions she placed on her in order to "straighten her out." Each day she felt more trapped and misunderstood, and the dreamed-of homecoming turned to ashes in her mouth. Her anxiety was staggering; she threatened to run off in the night and begged me to take her back. I turned a deaf ear to her pleadings at first, detecting the same controlling manipulation she often used to get her way, but when it was clear that the experiment was ill-fated, and she agreed to my conditions of regular therapy, medication, appropriate behavior, and no drugs, we booked her on the first available flight home.

For the next few months, Annie went along with our demands, but it was not long before her rage got the better of her, and she was back in the hospital. This time when the case worker informed me Annie was ready for discharge, I refused to take her home. After some finagling with the insurance company, she called me with one other option, a two-month stay in a group home for troubled teens. The facility had a fair reputation, but its main draw was a gifted therapist on staff who specialized in treating teens who had suffered any type of trauma.

Annie's prior hospital stays were mostly filled with group activities, a revolving door of psychiatrists, and almost no individual therapy. Grateful as I was for these brief hiatuses, they were no more than a sea wall against the tidal wave of her rages. Part of me felt callous for sending her to the group home, but another part of me had hardened toward her and hoped this more extreme treatment would have a more positive impact than any of the others had.

Annie lived at the group home for six weeks, sharing household duties and earning privileges along with the other housemates, a hard-core lot of struggling minors. Most had no stable home, and one arrived shackled in chains. A minivan transported Annie to and from school, where she was now in the eighth grade. Jean, the group home therapist, got right down to business, conducting frequent individual sessions with Annie, as well as weekly family sessions with all of us,

Mike and Joe included. There was an abundance of issues to wade through, everything from Mike's stern style of discipline to my own "enmeshed" parenting style, to conflicts with her brother, who was often forgotten amid the mayhem and was full of animosity. The topic that was still too tender for Annie to touch, though, was her second-grade experience with Sister Maria.

I was defensive and took exception to Jean's assessment of my relationship with Annie. Even though my identification with her symptoms had once been so extreme I could not distinguish where Annie left off and I began, I demurred because I felt the "enmeshed" label was too facile and convenient. I thought I had been careful to avoid placing either child in the role of confidante or burdening them with inappropriate personal matters. When Mike left, I made sure they knew there was no need to take care of me and that I was quite capable of carrying on alone as their parent. They also knew their father would always be nearby for support. But how could a mother not be enmeshed in her children's lives? I wondered; how could she not feel their joys and disappointments almost more than they did? As an adult, I frequently felt my own parents' emotions, sometimes to an uncomfortable degree. The night before my mother's final surgery, I could feel my soul resting in such deep communion with hers, so intimately woven in anxiety, hope, and prayer, that I lay awake churning with agita, feeling that I, in fact, *was* her. Whenever my father could not relax in a social setting, I, too, was ill at ease and could not take my mind off his acute discomfort. Now Jean implied there was something unhealthy and objectionable about this tendency of mine, and I was not sure how to respond.

In psychodynamic terms, enmeshment is the state of being from which "all children must wrest their sense of individual selfhood ... as a child develops, she begins to see that her mother is a separate being with her own thoughts and feelings. However, an emotionally deprived and depressed mother may feel threatened by her child's growing separation and unconsciously promote the enmeshment. The consequences can be severe, interfering with the child's ability to assert a separate identity" (Bialosky). I did not resonate with this symbiotic dyad of dependency. Though my childhood was not ideal, and my personality far from buoyant, I knew that, even unconsciously, I was not seeking to fetter my child to me.

However, I did believe there was something about the way Annie and I fit together that made our relationship particularly thorny and entangled. I *was* enmeshed with her in that I understood so much of what she experienced—the anxiety, isolation, OCD, depression, irritability, hypersensitivity—and could neither stanch the flow of my empathy for her nor tone down my emotional reactivity toward her. I had wanted a better life for her, one free from so much useless angst, but for better or worse, to some degree, our behavior was congenital, and we shared the same capacity for deep, soul-disturbing emotions. Daily life with Annie, though, was like tiptoeing through a minefield, and when her rage fed my rage, the enmeshment aborted, the walls went up, and I divorced myself from the emotional pain behind her fury. Boundaries were imperative. I had to learn to "detach with love," leave the spigot of empathy open just enough to acknowledge her suffering but not enough to drown in it, to withstand her rages without leaving permanent scars, to help her find her way but tend to myself, as well.

Jean also made passing reference to our "disorganized" attachment. She said there was nothing "wrong" with this but that it was just a good fact to know. In research, however, I discovered it meant that Annie could not rely on my consistently warm and reassuring presence, especially when confronted with any type of threat or discomfort. Children with this style of attachment might approach the parent for protection, but as they get closer, they pull away or even lash out at the parent to defend against the disappointment or hurt of an unresponsive or abusive parent. Consequently, their own behavior becomes unpredictable. Adults with a disorganized attachment to their own parents frequently repeat the pattern with their children and often have problems with depression, intimacy, and regulating their emotions.

Although my attachment to my own parents had surely become disorganized, I did not feel it was because I could not count on them to protect me. I was too withdrawn and inhibited to realize there was some glue missing between us or that there was any need to reach out to them. Instead, I expressed my discomfort in confused anger, before finally going inward and stuffing my wayward emotions almost completely. Despite this early peculiarity, I thought I had been a steady nurturing presence for Annie. Her rages often estranged us, but I did not think they were necessarily in reaction to me. Although I do not absolve myself from ways I contributed to Annie's problems, it also seemed there was always some fuel within her that was ready to combust.

Chapter 12

> "Rusticus pudor, bashfulness, flushing in the face,
> high color, ruddiness, are common grievances,
> which much torture many melancholy men, when
> they meet a man, or come in company of their
> betters, strangers [...] it exceeds, they think every
> man observes, takes notice of it: and fear alone will
> affect it, suspicion without any other cause."

The Anatomy of Melancholy, Robert Burton

One evening, as I sat with Annie in the drafty family meeting room of the psychiatric hospital, she looked at me with confusion in her eyes and told me she was "afraid of people." She could not comprehend why her face got so hot when someone looked directly at her, why she felt compelled to turn away and hide. She thought I would never understand such a thing, but I did, because it was the source of many of my own private humiliations. I hated to hear she was a hostage to self-consciousness as I had been, that she could not bear people looking at her, that she felt the urge to jump out of her skin in the most ordinary situations. Her admission reminded me of the embarrassing lengths I had gone to in my own life when confronted with unavoidable social roadblocks.

Though I knew panic attacks were a common occurrence for Annie, I was surprised that "social anxiety" had become a major handicap. I thought she had sidestepped this particular torment. Unlike me, she was not particularly shy or self-conscious; on the contrary, early on she enjoyed the limelight and craved attention. She dreamed of fame and pursued acting, dancing, and singing as possible pathways to glory. In first grade, she begged us to ship her off to a place called "Pop Hollywood Academy," somewhere in Los Angeles, which sounded like a mythical idyll of show business we were not sure even existed. In fourth grade, she performed a delightful Madonna-like solo in the school talent show, and I applauded her moxie, her pluck, her audacity. Her ability to throw herself into performance art was a joyfully outgoing way to distract herself from doom and gloom, but her powerful anxiety eventually won out, dousing that glorious youthful effervescence.

Anxiety thwarted most of Annie's ambitions. At two and three years old, she was full of spunk, champing at the bit to ride her brother's school bus, always game for the next adventure. One morning as I drove her to a toddler playgroup, she announced from her car seat that she planned to attend college in London someday and travel "all over the world." She had been graceful and fearless on the kindergarten and first-grade sports fields. In fact, we briefly thought we had a prodigy on our hands as we watched her tear down the pee-wee soccer field, scoring goal after goal, week after week. We were baffled, then, a few years later when that same in-domitable competitor stood rooted in place on the elementary school soccer field, afraid to stray beyond a five-foot radius for fear one of us would be struck by a fatal bolt of lightning or some other deadly calamity. It was the same threat of damn-ation and destruction if she transgressed some impossible-to-be-certain-of boundary, the same quintessential OCD fear.

It was hard to square those premature, almost cocky images of Annie with the teenager who quailed at the prospect of starting anything new. "Just go in and hold your head up high; you're as good as anyone else in there," I often told her, trying to boost her confidence as I dropped her off at the latest anxiety-producing undertaking. Her diffidence belied the brash creature she was at home, where she was all bluster and bravado. She never asked for, let alone accepted, a whit of help or advice—"I *know* how to do it! I *know* what to do!"—while her vast insecurities simmered just below the surface. Her perpetually worried expression, along with her incessant nail-biting and bleeding, almost chewed-to-the-bone cuticles, betrayed her. Belligerently attacking came more naturally to her than expressing naked vulnerability, but in those middle school years, so rife with opportunities for torment, I could still, on occasion, see the hurting child. It may be that I ascribe too much gravity to the consequences of commonplace adolescent setbacks, but such deep disappointments leveled at a time when she was struggling with towering anxiety and bullying were particularly severe sucker-punches.

When she was in sixth grade, for example, she felt she had a good chance of making both the volleyball team and the school play. The afternoon of the final cuts, she kept circling my computer, waiting for the official confirmation to roll out, already tasting victory. I, too, felt invested, anticipating a reason to celebrate, happily envisioning her healthy involvement in practices and rehearsals. But when the chosen lineups unfurled down my computer screen, she scrolled to the very last name on each list and realized hers was not among either of them. Her head drooped in stunned silence for a few seconds, and then she bolted from the room in choked tears.

I had never thought much about the exclusionary nature of extracurricular activities before then, but now it felt cruel and discriminatory to me. Yes, there were resilience-building benefits to surviving these disappointments, but Annie was not an ordinary adolescent, and I wished the teachers could know how those decisions affected her. She may have grown a slightly tougher skin after that, but she never again approached any endeavor without undiluted pessimism and self-doubt.

* * * * * *

Social anxiety disorder is essentially pathological shyness, a state more severe than the passing squalls of ordinary bashfulness, although they arise from the same bed of inborn temperament, family dynamics, early socialization, and life experiences. The disorder typically starts in childhood and early adolescence and can become chronic and incapacitating if not treated early, most promisingly with cognitive behavioral therapy and, sometimes, medication.

Social anxiety disorder (SAD) was first included in psychiatry's official reference guide, the DSM (*Diagnostic and Statistical Manual),* in 1980, naming it the third most common psychological disorder in the country, after depression and substance use disorder. Millions of people throughout the world suffer from social anxiety disorder, including approximately 7.1 percent of the US population. Individuals with SAD avoid interacting with other people because they anticipate being judged negatively. They intensely fear social situations, which make them acutely self-conscious and induce feelings of inferiority, anxiety, and panic. Social anxiety disorder can be specific, such as a single overriding fear of public speaking, or it can be pervasive and generalized, affecting almost every aspect of a person's life. Whether specific or general, individuals afflicted with SAD abhor the sensation of being watched, of holding court, of being the center of anyone's focused attention, always afraid of somehow embarrassing themselves, and constantly dreading the next SAD-inducing encounter.

As with all the psychiatric disorders, "sorting out nature and nurture, genes and environment can be a tortuous process" (Hollander and Bakalar). Both my parents would have scored high on any social anxiety meter, and I knew the odds favored the same for my own children; however, for Annie, there was also the tempering influence of Mike's more gregarious, outgoing nature, which she seemed to have inherited in good part.

Psychology professor Frank Bruno maintains that for those of us whose social anxiety has a particularly strong genetic component, we can learn to "dis-identify" from our parents, assert our personality independence from them, and make a conscious effort to cope with our inherent temperament. "Even if you are overly reserved and introverted, and even if this contributes to our phobias, you can cope with your inborn disposition," he claims. We can learn to lessen the genetic influence by implementing various coping strategies and through professional help—"One does not need to be ever the victim of oneself."

The mental health profession has been accused of "medicalizing" the personality trait of shyness; however, minimizing the legitimacy of SAD can be costly. With SAD, at some point, the gentle charm of shyness turns against us, and that shift can undermine our mental health. SAD sufferers may not present in emergency rooms with severe panic attacks because their physiological symptoms usually subside once they remove themselves from triggering situations, but the shame of SAD sticks to the psyche, and the obsessive dread and inclination to avoid meaningful life encounters insinuates itself into an individual's character. Small wonder, then, that only about 5 percent of people with social anxiety disorder seek treatment or that by the time they do, typically after no less than fifteen years of suffering, it is not only the discomfort of SAD that brings them through the professional's door. Studies show that between 50 and 80 percent of people with SAD also fall victim to any of the various co-morbid psychiatric conditions such as major depression, panic disorder, mood disorder, personality disorder, generalized anxiety disorder, substance use disorder, or eating disorder. And because SAD medications can exacerbate the symptoms of other psychiatric disorders, particularly bipolar disorder, an accurate reporting of symptomatology is essential to any diagnosis to avoid the dangerous effects of mixing contraindicated drugs.

* * * * * *

I can trace my own social-anxiety-generated metamorphosis back to the sixth grade when our Catholic school class was taught by a lay teacher named Mrs. Donohue. As with Sister Maria, Mrs. Donohue's tenure at the school lasted only one life-altering—to me—year.

In those days, the school faculty considered it prudent to separate the boys and girls when they reached the sixth grade, so for the next three years, we were safeguarded in our own female wing of the school. Forced to nurse our pre-teen crushes from afar, we threw furtive glances at the boys as we passed their half of the schoolyard each day. Occasionally, the boys *and* girls were invited to "mixers," which entailed herding us all down to the gymnasium in hopes that we might figure out the social mores on how to interact with the boys we had only just left behind in fifth grade. These were unfailingly stilted gatherings, and the two factions rarely commingled. When someone did migrate to the other side, approximately three hundred pairs of eyes watched in astonishment.

Before we started each school day, Mrs. Donohue lined us up in the corridor outside our classroom and pontificated on the moral obligation we had to act as "*ladies*," with "*maturity*," or, as she pronounced it, "ma—TUR—ity." Some of us exchanged eye rolls or giggled behind her back, but I was thrown off by her preachy, austere manner. She frightened me with her repeated warnings about how we ladies must be exemplary specimens of virtuous behavior *or else*. She was older than the teachers we were used to, with silvery-gray hair, and she wore tight button-down blouses, sometimes torn at the armpits. When she stood in the aisle next to my desk and stretched out her arm, I was repulsed by her unpleasant body odor. There were times she spoke to us about her son, who had been killed in a car crash, and I shuddered to think how unhappy her life must be.

It was at exactly this time that I was suddenly terrified to speak in class. I could not produce vocal sensations without sheer panic. Many nights I lay in bed trembling uncontrollably at the thought of being called upon the next day in class to answer a question or read a passage. At puberty, when girls, especially, experience a loss of self-esteem, I became, apparently overnight, so inhibited by the sound of my own voice that it was an absolute torment to me. That fear grew into a phobia of mammoth proportions, spawning OCD fears about germs, obsessive thoughts about guilt, and dictating my panicky avoidance of certain social situations ever since.

From the sixth grade on, any kind of public speaking has been nearly unendurable for me. I have fluctuated between specific and generalized SAD, with the fear of public speaking a lasting Achilles heel. The words "oral report" always struck the coldest kind of terror in my heart. I need only think of the times I heard a teacher, or anyone, say, "Let's go around the room so you can tell us a little something about yourselves," to recall my instant racing heart and violent urge to escape.

I suppose I was primed for this type of social dysfunction. Mrs. Donohue stirred up anxieties about what *ladies* did and did not do; she spoke in code about the dangerous influences we were up against, and I must have latched on to her mistrust of our adolescent instincts. I was also the same age my brothers were when they were involved in the shooting. I knew bad things happened, and no one talked about them afterward. The muted guilt I breathed in the air at home now permeated my life in and out of school as well. I was afraid of Mrs. Donohue's ambiguous messages, of doing something wrong, of causing my parents more grief. Though I tried to forget her, she had been a disastrous mentor for me that crucial year and left a lasting wound, just as Sister Maria had with Annie. While most girls in my class probably remember Mrs. Donohue as nothing more than a harmless kook, I transformed under her watch into the proverbial basket case. That teacher-student debacle was an uncanny foreshadowing of my daughter's own future undoing.

*　*　*　*　*　*

The social anxiety Annie and I share has the power to excise large portions of life and can be enough to spoil one's most cherished dreams. At the small, all-girls Catholic high school I attended, we were required to take two full courses of speech in our junior and senior year, the prospect of which terrified me more than anything in life. For the sole purpose of avoiding those classes, I concocted a drastic escape plan. I convinced my mother that this lovely school, which was a stone's throw away from the Verrazano-Narrows Bridge, where the sun set a burnt orange and scarlet on late wintry afternoons, where I was a respected varsity basketball player and had a close-knit group of friends, was not quite suitable for me, that I, in fact, preferred the company of less privileged peers at the huge public high school. I could not tell her the real reason I sought this change, that I was too anxious to face those classes. The principal called our home to offer help with tuition, thinking the obstacle was financial, but my mother graciously declined. And so I transferred to the larger school, where I was not required to take speech classes at all and where I merged blandly, safely, into the crowd.

I drifted away from that circle of friends, never having revealed the wild panic that drove me out, but I was drawn back on the evening of their senior graduation. I watched as these elegant graduates filed out the auditorium door into the soft summer dusk, resplendent in long white gowns, carrying bouquets of cascading red roses. How untroubled they all seemed! They exuded a confidence and joy foreign to me, and I thought how sad it was that I had not been able to open my mouth back then to ask for help, but the fears and phobias surrounding my social anxiety in those days were incapacitating and dominated my life.

* * * * * *

I relate one more regretful example of how social anxiety played out in my life: Before Annie was born, I had spent three years at night and weekend classes, and many thousands of dollars, training to become a court reporter. I painstakingly learned how to use the stenographic machine and how to interpret the inscrutable shorthand symbols, I also honed my grammar and punctuation skills, studied medical and legal terminology, and through countless hours of daily practice, committed the condensed keystrokes to muscle memory, which I later translated into the English language. This type of work had long intrigued me, and I thought I might have a knack for it, but I steered myself right into a brick wall. I was too far along in the program to turn back when I knew with certainty that I could not avoid the possibility of being asked to "read back" testimony, either in a courtroom or at a deposition in a lawyer's office. *Maybe it won't be all that bad,* I kept trying to reassure myself, *only a sentence now and then, two at the most,* but I had to finally confess to my husband that the stress of knowing I could be called upon at any moment to read aloud in front of strangers was too much for me. I was in my last trimester of pregnancy with Annie when I completed my internship with a law firm that seemed interested in taking me on as a fledgling reporter, but after I passed the final exam and officially graduated, I packed up my steno machine, stored it in the farthest corner of my closet, gave birth within months, and went back to mostly full-time motherhood.

For the next five years, I paid back that school loan each month with the same sense of failure and loss. It was yet one more stimulating, lucrative profession I would never have because of my intense anxiety. Even today, my fingers occasionally flutter in the air, reaching for the correct keystrokes for words I hear. That experience still speaks to me of who I am, who I have been, and how hard it can truly be to overcome one's fears.

There was only one time in my life when I encountered someone who seemed as socially anxious as I, and in the end, she acquitted herself with more aplomb than I ever did. We were in a graduate literature class together. I was a young newlywed at the time, taking night classes after working at my full-time secretarial job in a Manhattan ad agency. We never exchanged more than a few words. She always gravitated to the rear of the room, sitting close to the back wall, and rarely made eye contact with anyone. She hunched over guardedly in her chair, with her head slightly lowered, and I could usually see the hint of a smile on her face. It made me feel less alone in my anxiety to see that she never raised her hand or contributed to class discussions. I presumed that, like me, she enjoyed the emotional depth and undemanding company of the authors we studied. After observing her all semester, I wrote her a card with a brief note of commiseration and encouragement, which I planned to give her on the final night of class.

As our culminating project, we were required to give an oral presentation, which, of course, I was dreading. Up until that point, I had not heard her speak a single word out loud, but when her turn came to present, she sailed through her delivery, giving a calm and clever recitation on her favorite author of the semester, Virginia Woolf, while I, on the other hand, sputtered and sweated and choked my way through a terse report on Joseph Conrad's *The Secret Sharer,* another doppelganger-themed novella of a timid man's emotional journey. I was too ashamed of having underestimated her ability and by my own poor performance to give her that card. I never saw my SAD twin again, but I knew she would fare better in many ways than I would, that she had a certain strength she could rely on. If any words of encouragement had been exchanged that night, they more rightly should have been dispatched from her to me.

Chapter 13

> "… I was washed over with complicated feelings
> from past and present—love, embarrassment,
> rejection, fear. Then, in the middle of this chaos,
> a huge Voice boomed out through the darkness.
> 'You must die!' Other Voices joined in.
> 'You must die! You will die!'"
>
> *The Quiet Room, Lori Schiller and Amanda Bennett*

In the spring of Annie's sixth-grade year, we learned that her psychological troubles had given rise to a worrying new symptom. It is difficult to think back on that night dispassionately or without grief. I had been lying in bed reading late one evening when Annie came into my room and crawled into bed beside me. She was distraught and could hardly speak. *"I'm hearing voices,"* she said. My heart dropped. *Oh, no. No, no, no. Not this,* I silently pleaded to myself. Then she revealed more. The voices were threatening to harm her and take her away. She also said she was "seeing things" but would not elaborate. She feared she was "going crazy," and I saw the terror and shame in her eyes. I felt such pity for her, and at the same time, I was frightened, my mind reeling with the dreaded implications of "hearing voices." As she sidled up closer to me, I held her, tried to reassure her she was okay, and then uttered, *"No wonder you act the way you do, with all that going on in your head!"*

I called Mike, who lived two blocks away from us, to tell him what happened. We had remained good friends, and he rushed over to try to comfort Annie, but neither of us knew where to turn. Therefore, we acted in accordance with any other medical emergency, and by the next morning, we were on our way to another psychiatric hospital. Annie was calmer in the light of day and seemed to look forward to the hospital admission, which I assumed was because she would feel safer from the voices there. With the hospital staff, she was stoic and forthcoming about the voices. When a worker came to take her to the locked ward, I found it hard to leave her in that barren setting, but we felt the voices were a development that required professional intervention. However, that hospitalization proved no better or worse than the last, another holding pattern of rest, group therapy, and safety monitoring before reentering the outside world. The one notable difference this time was the class of drug Annie was prescribed to address her voices—"antipsychotics." It was her frightening foray into these difficult-to-tolerate, powerful, and controversial medications.

✳ ✳ ✳ ✳ ✳

The night Annie first told me about the voices was my initiation into the complex world of hearing voices. Though I could usually put myself in her shoes psychologically, this was uncharted territory. It seemed at first beyond my ken to imagine what hearing voices might be like, yet I remembered how, in my early 20s, I happened upon the semiautobiographical novel *I Never Promised you a Rose Garden* by Joanne

Greenberg and the anonymously penned *Autobiography of a Schizophrenic Girl.* These books are still on my shelves today, their pages studded with marginalia and stocked with sloppily underlined sentences and paragraphs that resonated with meaning for me back then. I remember accessing these authors' worlds hesitantly but then feeling strangely attuned to the emotional subtext. I recall having the sense that I had narrowly escaped descending to that same level of alienation, having a distinct impression that had my anxieties gotten much further apace, I would have been as lost at sea as these two writers once were. As Elyn Saks articulates in *The Center Cannot Hold,* I felt "how easily I could have been any one of them. How easily I could have slipped beneath the waves and simply never come back up again."

Now, suddenly confronted with my daughter's very real and distressing symptom of hearing voices, I sought knowledge and personal stories like these. While Annie was still in the hospital, I scouted the mental health literature in search of solace and struck gold one afternoon at Barnes & Noble when I discovered a poignant account of a young woman's struggle with voices entitled, *The Quiet Room: A Journey Out of the Torment of Madness,* by Lori Schiller and Amanda Bennett. Lori's voices started when she was seventeen, at least five years later than Annie's, and she waged a private war with them for another twelve years before achieving any measurable relief. Lori's harrowing journey became an atlas and guide for me, and I admired and appreciated the courage it took for her to write that book. In the end, Lori was helped by the drug clozapine, but as her psychiatrist, Dr. Jane Doller, states, "I believe that the turning point for Lori occurred long before clozapine came on the scene. It happened during the early months of her final hospitalization when she finally began to face the illness head-on, when she finally became able to say, 'I'm very sick. I need help.' It was only then that she was able to take the risk of becoming truly involved in her treatment, of opening up to others about what she was feeling, and of beginning to connect with other people."

When Annie returned home from the hospital, I asked her, as gently as I could, to give me an idea of what the voices said to her, but she covered her eyes with her hands and whimpered, *"No! I don't want to talk about that! It's too horrible!"* She was only twelve, and I could see it was torture for her to think about the voices, let alone tell me what they said, but when I persisted, she grudgingly revealed a few phrases that were almost identical to the things Lori's voices said—*"Go die! Kill yourself! You deserve to rot in hell."* I did not have the heart to pry further, but I suggested to her that there might be some value in writing these things down. She wanted no part of that, which I understood, yet I knew it had been a crucial step for Lori. In *The Quiet Room*, Lori writes:

> *I hated telling anyone about the Voices. They were too terrible, too frightening. They would kill anyone I told about them. They would kill me if I told. I couldn't tell her (the psychiatrist). But I wanted to tell her. I wanted her to know. I wanted to please her. I wanted to do what was right. So I decided to write to her. Over one evening, I wrote it all down. I wrote down everything that was in my head, all the sounds and noises, and meaningless phrases. All the endless repetitions of "To die!" All the hatred, the bile, everything foul the Voices had said to me and about me. The next morning, I stuffed into her hands the transcript of my head. And now she knew. I waited for her to die. I waited for her to laugh. I wanted her to turn on me in disgust. But she didn't. Instead, she was grateful.*

I knew Annie was too young to face those phantoms, to articulate the foul things they said, or bravely "out" them as

Lori had. Now that she had told me about the voices, and now that she had been roundly pathologized for them in the hospital, she refused to talk about them, and I had to tread ever more lightly around the topic at all.

* * * * * *

Annie's voices were classified by the psychiatrists as "auditory hallucinations," sensory perceptions created by the mind and occurring in a vacuum, without any auditory stimulus in the external environment. In the medical world, they are significant mostly in their indication of "psychosis"—a break with reality. Psychosis is also a broad term, encompassing not only auditory hallucinations but other sensory perceptions that others in the same physical space do not experience, like visions, tastes, smells, and tactile sensations. Other types of psychosis include thought disorders (delusions) and "catatonia," the condition in which the body no longer moves or responds to the external world. Psychotic experiences can lead to varying degrees of personality change, impairments in social abilities, and challenges in everyday functioning.

Before a primary psychiatric disorder can be diagnosed, physiological causalities like central nervous system diseases, brain injuries, and drug-related emergencies must first be ruled out. It was the other, more psychological risk factors for psychosis, such as stress and childhood trauma, that stamped Annie's condition with the psychiatric label. In fact, the more we learned about auditory hallucinations, the more they seemed like the natural next step in the progression of her profound dis-ease with herself, the farther end of the continuum of symptoms and experiences which externalized her extreme emotional agitation.

In modern society, hearing voices is probably considered the most sensational feature of mental illness, the one common striking detail mentioned in any public profile of a seriously disturbed individual. Even professionals in the mental health field seem disquieted at the mention of voices. One psychiatrist, after a 90-minute intake interview with Annie, said she could not treat her as an outpatient because her voices posed "too much of a risk." Annie had again been forthright with her answers in the hope that medication would give her some relief, but the doctor seemed only to care whether her voices were "commanding," the type of voices that direct a person to either self-harm or harm others. I understood her concern (the liability issues), but I was furious that after putting Annie through this extensive interrogation, she left her twisting in the wind, feeling like a dangerous criminal who needed to be locked down.

A great deal in psychiatry rides on this deceptively simple question. If, for instance, the voices are more benign, they might be considered the product of a passing stressful life event—what the psychiatric literature calls a "brief reactive psychosis." The doctor, in this case, might prescribe a mild medication to tide the individual over until the acute phase of suffering subsides. However, once the "commanding" feature of voices is established, the psychiatrists Annie saw invariably mobilized their first-line drugs to "take care of them," as we were often told. The only challenge for the doctor at that point is to mull over which of the older "typical" antipsychotics or newer "atypical" drugs might best annihilate them. But it was never that easy. The psychiatrists threw everything in their arsenal at the voices to no avail. I was beginning to wonder whether snuffing out the voices was a realistic goal or even necessary, for, by that time, I was reading that auditory hallucinations, in and of themselves, were not the true earmark of psychosis, but rather it was the inability to distinguish them from reality.

The psychiatrists Annie saw were busy and ran a tight ship. Once the initial intake interview was performed, their appointments never exceeded the 15 – 20 minutes required for "medication checks," which did nothing to inspire a full-bodied relationship. Constraints imposed by insurance companies reinforce these practices, but in general, psychiatrists steer clear of "issues," abstain from therapeutic analysis, and avoid any appearance of "collusion" with their patients' hallucinations lest they lend credence to them or embolden voice hearers to act on their voices' commands. As medical doctors, psychiatrists are searching for an efficient cure, or at least a significant reduction in symptoms, and they, therefore, delegate talk therapy, the softer, slower, less scientific side of the healing process, to psychologists and social workers.

Psychiatrist Lewis Mehl-Madrona states in his book, *Healing the Mind through the Power of Story,* that modern medicine, including psychiatry, aspires to an "objective distancing," and the "removal of human interactions is central to this movement." In this milieu, "lip service is paid to psychotherapy." Psychiatric medications give "the illusion of the pristine nature of drug therapy, a clean intervention in which the messiness of emotions and of unbearable affect can be ignored." He also maintains that people "diagnosed with depression who subscribe to the biological story can relinquish much of their need to participate in any conversation about themselves, except about how the medications are affecting them." Similarly, Annie was never encouraged by psychiatrists to look at the voices as being in any way connected to her, as being a bellwether of her emotional Sturm and Drang. The psychiatrists she saw considered the specifics of voice hearing irrelevant, something better left outside their consultation rooms.

Yet still, if there was a psychiatrist who could prescribe a medication to grant Annie's old life back, to dispel those shadows from her psyche, I was all for it. Despite what I knew about treating the whole person, not just symptoms, we would persevere, as Lori had, until we found a medication that worked. It was, after all, the heyday of "medical-model" psychiatry, when better, more effective medications arrived on the scene all the time. And was it not one of those still-experimental, last-resort drugs that finally saved Lori, even though it required continuous blood tests and legal consent because of its many black box warnings? Though I was not ready to sacrifice the rest of Annie's health to conquer the voices, I hoped that a Prozac-like wonder drug might come along which could vanquish them, the same way clozapine had taken down Lori's.

But the medications never helped or even came close, and the side effects were crippling. When Annie was in the hospital, she sometimes falsely told the doctors that the voices were gone because the absence of them was considered proof of successful treatment, and she could then be discharged. By the time she was living at the group home when she was in the eighth grade, the resident psychiatrist increased her dose of the antipsychotic Risperdal to the point that she was incapacitated—by the medicine, not the voices. My heart ached when I visited her and watched her slowly shuffle toward me, her arms hanging limply at her sides. Her eyes were two impenetrable pools of darkness, and I tried hard not to focus on the dispiriting tremor in her hands. She struggled to form thoughts and speak, and the sight of her left me weeping in the car long after we said goodbye.

Here is Annie's perspective on that time, written many months after she was discharged:

Annie: I am lifeless, grossly over-medicated, and barely able to communicate. Personal hygiene is long gone. I fall asleep brushing my teeth or slump to the floor of the shower in an exhausted stupor. I watch my lethargic, decrepit body from above, a girl's feet shuffling slowly,

slowly through a pair of dingy doors, pointed in the direction of a nearby sofa. There are other people in the scene, my mother and father, people speaking in hushed murmurs.

The sense of viewing myself from above continues. A voice hisses, "You're already dead, see? Look at that disgusting creature, you're a waste, a monster." I wince. Prisoner to a defunct brain, I long to crack this head of mine wide open, to pluck the demons out one by one, finally reclaim the ravaged mind I once called my own. A room is assigned, and a top bunk given to me. Now it is time to say goodbye. There are tears in my parents' eyes as they tell me once more, "You cannot come home right now. It is not safe. You need help, Annie." Suddenly I am aware, cognizant of what is happening, and I am a wild animal, thrashing, trapped. Take me home, I want to go home!

Days later, a small woman beckons me into her office. Her hair is a frizzy mop of curls, not unlike my own when I was young. She gently tells me her name is Jean and that we will be working together during my time in the group home. I am tired, so tired, but she is nice, and in here I am safe. I sit for a while, silent, and Jean does not push but sits quietly too. Finally, a voice speaks, slowly, barely loud enough to be heard, and I am surprised to find it is my own, pleading and unfamiliar: "I want to go home." Jean sighs deeply, and I register genuine sadness in her eyes, responding, "I know sweetheart, I know."

My time spent in the group home is nightmarish, lonely. The few moments of light that shine through exist only within Jean's office, where I am comforted by the love only a dog can give. Jean has a new puppy, Maggie, and the little King Charles's snores have come to be a calming lullaby during our sessions, muffled and rhythmic, constant, unchanging. Time after time, I sink into Jean's familiar couch, still comatose from the medication but finding temporary solace in stroking Maggie's silky, long fur. As I pet Maggie, I am reminded of my own animals back home and quickly notice hot tears beginning to accumulate, threatening to spill over with one false move. Don't think about it, don't think about it. I fight to stay awake, speak until the words will not come anymore, the three of us together, twice a week, before I must leave and fight to survive another day.

I repeatedly urged the psychiatrist to lower the dose of Risperdal, but he disagreed that it was excessive and instead recommended increasing it. Before Annie left the group home, he reluctantly agreed to reduce the medication, while making it clear it was against his better judgment. This was the second time in my life that I had stood by helplessly while my daughter suffered at the hands of an unyielding authority figure, and I vowed I would never again give anyone that kind of power.

* * * * * *

The voices assailed Annie throughout her middle school years. Still on the reduced dose of Risperdal, she frequently fell asleep in class or on her counselor's couch. The staff was kind and accommodating, and they tried their best not to hold her back from graduating, despite her poor attendance and nominal schoolwork. There were days I had to physically pull her out of bed to catch the bus, but she somehow managed to cross the finish line. We assured the school administrators that Annie would be in better shape by the fall; we would see that she remained in regular therapy and, with the help of a psychiatrist, would spend the summer titrating her medications.

Mike and I could not imagine how she would cope with the social and intellectual demands of our huge public high school, so we touted the virtues of "alternative" schools, thinking they would be less intimidating and better equipped to handle her psychological needs. However, when we toured several of these promising schools in our area, Annie said she could not envision herself at any of them. Instead, she chose placement in the "Emotional Support" (ES) program at the public high school because she wanted to remain in as "normal" an environment as possible, and we viewed her decision as an optimistic sign.

Over the course of that summer, Annie weaned off Risperdal completely, and I watched her gradually emerge from that unnatural state of quietude. She told me how weird and isolated the medication had made her feel and how nearly impossible it was to accomplish the simplest physical or mental task because of its deadening effect. She never wanted to go back to "that place" again, she said, but through-out her high school years, the psychiatrists kept at it. When she mentioned "voices," they inevitably added one more drug to the cocktail she was already on for anxiety, OCD, and depression. Once the new antipsychotic prescription was filled, she would stare at the bottle but ultimately refrain from taking the pills. Her experience with these drugs had left her too traumatized to try them again, and, to a certain extent, out of necessity, she was learning to live with the voices. I was always secretly relieved by her decision, dreading the faraway look in her eyes, watching the life force siphon out of her as the medication took effect. But if Annie's voices could be eradicated this way, I did not want to, and tried not to, interfere with her right to choose that option.

Free of the antipsychotics, Annie made a go of it at the public high school. The Emotional Support Program usually consisted of a cast of shaky students, all struggling to get back on the educational track after any number of personal or behavioral problems. Psychiatric diagnoses were not impor-tant there; no one cared whether she had bipolar, borderline personality, schizoaffective, PTSD, or any other disorder. The non-traditional setting suited her, and she got along well with both teachers and students. She was cooperative and respectful, commiserated with her peers' underlying issues, and often helped defuse tense situations which occasionally broke out among the more volatile students. In her junior year, Annie's guidance counselor designed a mentoring opportunity for her to capitalize on her budding peer support strengths, and once a week, she was bused to the middle school so she could meet with students who were struggling with their own difficulties.

Annie's two ES teachers were also her "case workers," and eventually they became more like friends. The school permitted them a wide latitude of motivational strategies, which included plenty of humor, inveigling, and coddling, as well as some straight talk about just getting "your shit together." But while she was grateful that her fellow students' more overt behavioral problems kept the focus off her own more inward ones, the teachers and students sometimes wondered why she was in the ES program at all. She seemed "fine" to them. At these times, Annie got angry that her troubles were minimized and that she felt the need to justify her place there. Although she had agreed to these downsides of the ES placement, she was often critical of its "squeaky-wheel" mentality, and I had to occasionally email her teachers to remind them of the full scope of symptoms Annie dealt with each day. I knew they were not trained psychologists and that especially a phenomenon like hearing voices was outside their bailiwick, but it was helpful for them to remember the gigantic effort it took for her to simply remain in school and concentrate on the task in front of her.

The ES program did make generous accommodations for Annie's anxiety by allowing her to leave classes and decompress in the ES lounge whenever she needed to. The teachers provided her extra time with assignments and tests and offered ample tutoring and counseling. Although she performed well enough on standardized tests, she never liked school and had a proven disability in math. She was also missing several years' worth of foundational learning because of her mental health challenges and hospitalizations during the middle school years. As time went on and she was able to pursue more electives, though, she distinguished herself in art, literature, and psychology courses. She wrote thoughtful essays and created vignettes filled with vivid characters and dialogue. In senior psychology, she authored and illustrated a children's book on body dysmorphia, which the teacher kept as a model for future classes and said showed exceptional sensitivity and insight.

At the crowded biannual IEP meetings (Individualized Education Plan), where we met with administrators, guidance counselors, teachers, and support workers, Annie was repeatedly encouraged to break through the confines of the ES program, but she pushed back hard, which made for some heated debates. The goal of the ES program was to "mainstream" students as soon as possible, but she fended off these more populated classes where the academic expectations were higher, and the social dynamics made her nervous. If there was a pep rally or other boisterous event, she peered through a small observation window near the ES room, which enabled her to still feel connected to the flow of high school life. Though the ES room remained her home base all four years, that public school went a long way toward normalizing the direction her life had taken. By the time she strode out onto the graduation field as a senior, she had assimilated herself into the larger whole of the student body and accepted her diploma with pride. She had managed to stay out of the hospital those four years; she was also in weekly therapy, on small doses of medication, and had a part-time job at a children's party facility.

When the time came for Annie to apply to colleges, I knew there was little chance she would go away to school, but we took the tours anyway. There was one school whose freshman dorm was located right next to the mental health building. The school was also smaller and closer to home than the others, which I hoped she would find comforting, and I encouraged her to give it a try. She was accepted at that school and several others, but she decided to stay local and attend the community college. The reason she gave for not going away was that she "could not handle the social scene." Again, I understood implicitly but tried to convince her to go anyway.

I, too, had gone to a community college after high school, despite my high grades and college acceptances. I rationalized to others that going away to school "just wasn't for me" rather than admit I would be overwhelmed by the expectations—the heavy workload, public speaking assignments, the party atmosphere, acclimating to new personalities, the general give-and-take it took to fit in. The stakes were too high. I knew I was vulnerable to psychological stress and so I never seriously considered it. For many years the fact that I did not go away to college bothered me because I knew I was not up to it. Touring those college campuses with Annie brought back how much I had missed, how many opportunities to a fuller life I had forfeited, and how much she, too, would likely miss.

Annie lasted one semester at the community college and then worked a series of jobs in retail, at a supermarket, at a doggie daycare center, as an embroiderer, at a hair salon, at a bakery, as a school aide, as a hospital patient transporter, in restaurants, always balancing her anxiety level with the tasks of employment. She considered herself "too stupid" to earn a college degree and found it difficult to commit to one path over another because she disliked the confining feeling it gave her. During these years, she also experienced the joys and sorrows of at least two serious romances with likable young men, and her world enlarged by seeing it through their eyes. She was learning how to compromise with another person, as well as how to restrain her furies. But there were personal crises as well, near hospitalizations, bleak periods of depression, alarming rages and panic attacks, voices, visions, and despair.

Chapter 14

"When the unconscious erupts at midlife, what first
comes most strongly to the fore are rejected pieces
of personality that were left undeveloped and cast
aside sometime in the past, for one reason or
another, in the rapid movement forward of personal
history. Life still clings to them. And actually
the seeds of the future lie in these neglected figures,
which now return and call for restoration
and attention."

In Midlife, Murray Stein

While I was frequently caught up in the maelstrom of Annie's tribulations, I was also more absorbed in my life apart from her. I was more clearheaded and content after having plummeted so low during Annie's second-grade year. I had gained some perspective on the porous frontier of pain between us and, in the intervening years, had sought to reclaim myself and reckon as much as possible with my limitations. Alas, some of my character traits were too deeply embedded and beyond my ameliorating powers, but with medication and therapy, my social anxiety eased, and I was a less passive spectator to my life.

I found myself responding to long-neglected stirrings in my soul. As I sat in a meeting at Annie's middle school one evening in which the music teachers demonstrated the various instruments available for our children to study, I was so moved by the rich, mellow resonance of the viola, I determined I would take up the instrument myself, which I did a few months later. I had also been pursuing my second master's degree, but when I returned to my studies after falling so ill, I not only enjoyed the purposeful inquiry into Catholicism but savored the pure love of learning, desiring to read as many classic works in the humanities as possible before I died. I landed a more satisfying job coordinating volunteer programs, pushing myself by interacting with numerous people each day. Volunteer work also called to me personally, and I began spending time, first, with psychiatric patients and then, later, with dying patients, impressed by the nobility of lives well-lived or those marked by suffering. I felt I might have something to offer these most vulnerable individuals, if nothing more than an open heart toward their troubles.

After my separation from Mike, however, I fell into a deep grief. Though the demise of the marriage was instigated by crises with Annie, other personal issues had surfaced, which equally contributed to its downfall. I knew the breakup was for the best, but I mourned the loss of the ideal partnership marriage represented, with all its comforts and privileges of mutual support, and I felt tremendous guilt and regret over my participation in the relationship's fracture. Annie's therapist agreed to see me for an emergency visit during the worst of this bereavement. She was a companionable, grandmotherly type, and I will never forget the way she spoke to me that brisk fall afternoon when I came apart in her office. It was not with the professional objective tone of the therapist, but like a caring mother or friend who could see right through to the best part of me. I sent her a letter afterward describing how that conversation had been one of the most meaningful of my life—"*When I so wrenchingly unburdened the pain, guilt, and sadness in my soul, you lifted me up with compassion, acceptance, and validation. You said <u>exactly</u> the things I needed to hear, with true sincerity. Shortly after that, I felt 'forgiven' somehow, as if, through you, God understood that I had tried my best, given my limitations. My failures and imperfections were not cause for the extraordinary shame and self-blame I felt. I am always able to revisit in my mind how you spoke to me, and, so far, it has never failed to soothe and console me.*"

* * * * * *

I began to search for support in other places, too, imagining there must be more parents like me out there, hunting for refuge and guidance. When Annie reached the middle school years and each day brought a further test of my fortitude, I was fortunate to find the B.I.L.Y. group ("Because I Love You"), a network of families struggling under assorted burdens with their loved ones. These family members commiserated and empathized with me. During group meetings, I lamented my shattered family and despaired over my suffering, out-of-control daughter, and in turn, they helped refocus my pain and frustration by delineating ways I could take responsibility—but not blame. They bolstered my strength to endure the tough times and empowered me to sympathize with my daughter but disengage enough to allow her to take ownership of her problems and determine her own path to recovery.

There were also important practical suggestions they gave me, like recommending we apply for state financial aid (Medical Assistance), which enabled us to obtain the services of a mental health agency that provided us "family-based" therapy for two years at no cost. The B.I.L.Y. group also connected me with NAMI (National Alliance on Mental Illness), an organization that sponsored an educational series of classes I attended for families and caregivers of children and adolescents living with mental illness. But while the B.I.L.Y. group was my first teacher and ally, the catalyst for so much positive change, I parted company with them after one year. Most of the B.I.L.Y. families were more acculturated to the realities of substance use disorder than to mental health issues, and while there were principles of that no-nonsense approach I needed to impose with Annie, more often, it was misaligned with the primary challenges she faced. Yet this, too, was a valuable lesson.

The mental health agency we worked with, Child and Family Focus, was our ballast for the two years following Annie's first hospitalization. Twice a week, they sent a team of a therapist and social worker to our home, once to work with Annie by herself and then with all four of us as a family. These two young, enthusiastic women saw her through several more hospitalizations, the six weeks at the group home, school meetings, and psychiatrist appointments. They ensured that crisis plans were in place and that we never felt alone amid the bedlam. They gained Annie's trust, helped her find ways to manage her anxiety, supported her in any goals she set for herself, created treatment plans, kept track of medications, offered respite care for Annie if we needed it, provided transportation to work when I had no car, treated me and all the other mothers they worked with to a weekend retreat, and when the time came for Annie to transition to the step-down branch of the agency ("wraparound support"), they took us out for dinner and presented us with a check to cover six months' worth of future therapy visits for Annie because her psychologist, Jean from the group home, did not yet take insurance for outpatients.

Annie developed a great affection for that team. She wrote a letter of gratitude to them, which she read aloud during their final home visit. From upstairs, I could hear them crying and laughing together. I wondered how we would manage without them, but within two weeks of their departure, the Child and Family Focus wraparound team came onboard, providing both Annie and me with "peer support partners" and the whole family with a continuous forum to deal with ongoing issues and devise problem-solving strategies. Our work with this team was less personally therapeutic for Annie than it had been with the family-based team, but their reassuring presence buttressed her through much of her high school years. Overall, the Child and Family Focus organization was a godsend to us and a revelation of the valuable and innovative work occurring in the mental health field by caring professionals.

Chapter 15

> "If you want to understand voice hearing or any
> complex psychological phenomenon, you must
> ultimately, no matter where else you choose to look,
> make the long pilgrimage to the oracle:
> the voice hearer himself."
>
> *Muses, Madmen, and Prophets, Daniel B. Smith*

In that first year when Annie began hearing voices, Mike and I attended a presentation on auditory hallucinations held at a behavioral health hospital not far from our home. The presenters gave a short introduction on the phenomenon and then handed each of us a pair of earphones, along with a small cassette player and tape of simulated "voices." Next, we each received a different list of tasks to perform in various locations throughout the hospital as we listened to our tapes and navigated our way through the building. The purpose of the exercise was to obtain an authentic feel for what the experience of hearing voices was actually like. I set about my route, determined to ignore the voices and stay focused on the tasks, but when the group later debriefed, we all commented on how difficult, scary, and demeaning it felt to follow our instructions while being berated by the voices.

The simulation had been a commendable effort in consciousness-raising, and by the end of the session, we knew more about the experience than when we started, but from everything Annie had told me and everything I had read about hearing voices, I knew it was a vast trivialization of the real thing. But despite this drawback, the activity of the voices on that tape—the alterations in tone, character, number of voices, and content—made an impression on me and is still probably the closest I am likely ever to approach the cacophony in Annie's head.

Annie's voices are her private experience, and I can never completely understand what living with them must be like, but she has entrusted me to try to "do some good" with them, maybe help shed light on and humanize this stigmatizing topic, or perhaps provide a modicum of succor and solidarity to other families. She is a young woman now, twenty-five as of this writing, living her life and grappling with many of the same issues other young adults her age do. The voices are still with her, unshakable, fluctuating with the intensity of her stress. Objectively, I am fascinated by the way her mind works, why the voices came to be, how they behave, and how she lives with them; subjectively, I am filled with untold sympathy for her and am in awe of the courage and strength she demonstrates each day of her life.

Hearing voices is a little-understood phenomenon, and the statistics disprove its apparent uniqueness. Overall, studies show that across the world, between 4 and 10 percent of people hear voices at any given time. A recent analysis conducted by researchers in the Netherlands broke that number down into the following categories of voice hearers: 12.7% of children, ages 5-12; 12.4% of adolescents, ages 13-17; 5.8% of adults, ages 18-60; and 4.5% of adults, ages 60 and over. The

Understanding Voices website (UV), produced at Durham University in England, states that voices can sometimes arise in response to medical problems such as acute fever or epilepsy, or in response to "life stresses, such as poor sleep, loneliness, and emotional distress." They can also be "triggered by trauma, such as the death of a close family member or friend, bullying, neglect, and physical or sexual assault." For most children and adolescents, as the source of stress and anxiety resolves, the voices fade away, but for others, like Annie, they become an intrinsic part of their identity. Learning to accept the voices is the herculean task for this population of voice hearers.

The voices were extraordinary, in their way. They were not like thoughts, which are soft and have no volume; they were obstreperous, not to be denied. They, too, were like ghosts in that I could not see them but only divine them by the turmoil they fomented in Annie. They were ne'er-do-wells she could not get rid of; cloak-and-dagger was their stock-in-trade. They were tormentors and torturers, testing the limits of her sanity, blackmailing her into submission if she breached their trust. They were rude and obscene, taunting her with insults and foul language. They were nosy, intruding on her private thoughts, and gossipy, prattling on about trifles. They were nasty and mean, loved to trip her up while she was working, socializing or trying to pay attention in class, calling her name from various corners of a room, just to confuse and embarrass her, which made it hard for her to "prioritize" what she heard. They were hecklers, mocking her and others at every turn. They were loafers, murmuring nonsensical chatter, lazy background static. They were boors, sniping at what she or anyone else around her was doing, wearing, or saying. They were male, female, and genderless. The qualities of the voices, what they sounded like to Annie, bore no resemblance to her own voice. They were entertainers and comedians, amusing themselves in comical asides and other mischief, sometimes even joking with her. They were loquacious and spoke gib-berish, riffing on everything they heard or saw, from the word "green" someone just uttered to the refrain from a song on the car radio. In addition to these "regular" voices, Annie also heard other sounds the rest of us did not hear, things like banging doors, shrill whistles, animal sounds, music, maniacal laughter, and screaming. Occasionally I jested, *"What's going on with the crew up there?"* *"Oh, you don't want to know!"* she would answer.

I asked Annie once why she thought the voices fluctuated so much, and she had this to say:

> **Annie:** *Loud noises are a trigger. The voices get even louder, and if there are too many loud noises, the voices will stay loud for a while. If anything about death comes up, they'll start chattering about death. Claustrophobia bothers me. The voices get louder in small spaces ... I feel trapped and can't function ... I feel like I can't breathe, and I get paranoid. The voices will start talking about how people hate me and ask me if I've heard what they're saying about me. Crowds are a trigger, homework and school used to be triggers, social events, family gatherings ... all things of that nature.*

Falling asleep at night was another Sisyphean task for her. The quieter Annie got, the more likely the voices were to rise in pandemonium. She kept the radio on loud at her bedside, kept the light on beside her, and kept her windows wide open even in the dead of winter, any physical sensation to distract her from the voices' commotion. Medications sometimes helped ease her into slumber, but they left her groggy and out of sorts the next morning. During high school, she began taking long showers with the radio on to literally drown out the voices. Reading, television, and knitting could be calming diversions for her, but, as she told me once, the struggle not to run out screaming in the streets was never less than exhausting. The focus of her days, therefore, was modest yet beyond most people's comprehension—to survive the continual onslaught of the voices without yielding to despair. However, despite that dissonance in her head, she was, in most other respects, a typical teenager, up on the latest music and fashion, experi-menting with makeup and hairstyles, and eager to obtain her driver's license. Her boyfriend at the time was kind and supportive, but she often wondered, *"What is he doing with me? I'm crazy!"*

* * * * * *

In the fall of 2012, I attended a different kind of hearing voices event, this one sponsored by NAMI and featuring a presentation by a Scotsman named Ron Coleman. The flyer said he would speak about his own experiences hearing voices. I had never met another person with the "lived experience" of hearing voices and was eager to hear what he had to say. Before the event got underway, I was browsing through the books and CDs spread along the side table when I overheard the gentleman next to me speaking with someone with a thick Scottish accent. When the opportunity arose, I nervously stepped forward and asked if he was Ron Coleman and if it was true that he heard voices. He casually nodded. I asked if he still heard voices, and he nodded again, adding, *"But I only listen to them for a short while in the evenings."* I told him that my daughter was also a voice hearer, but before we had the chance to chat further, he was called to the stage. I realized then that I had not been expecting someone so completely rational, friendly, and approachable and that I was not immune to the stereotypes many of us have in mind when we hear that a person "hears voices."

Ron was articulate, witty, and charmingly disheveled-looking, and he spoke warmly of his wife and many children. He revealed details of his early traumas and described his years in psychiatric institutions, but the main purpose of his visit was to raise awareness around the phenomenon of hearing voices as part of the "diversity of the human experience." Ron explained that voices most often occur in a person's life after experiencing some type of trauma. Whether the trauma is emotional, physical, or sexual in nature, he said, voices are a normal human reaction to the overwhelming psychological stress induced by that trauma. He emphasized that they are not a sign of "madness" but rather a meaningful way human beings cope with their extreme feelings of powerlessness and helplessness. Voices thus do not come out of nowhere; they arise within a social and emotional context. As any victims of trauma will attest, they did not choose the terrible thing that happened—it was forced on them against their will. Their world was blown apart, and voices were like shrapnel after the explosion. Voices can also be likened to broken slivers of a mirror, reflecting a kaleidoscope of distorted self-images to the voice hearer. According to Ron Coleman, those pieces need to be put back together and made meaning of. Voices, he said, hold special messages that the voice hearer cannot afford to ignore.

Ron made a distinction between the traumatic event—*what happened* to the voice hearer—and the voices themselves, which are the *consequence* of what happened. While the trauma was no doubt a horrendous event, he maintained that it is not necessarily the primary problem for the voice hearer. *Emotions* are what fuel the voices, and when human beings cut themselves off from the emotions that naturally flow from traumatic events, they profoundly disrupt the healthy processing of the trauma. For Ron, it all starts with one question, *"What happened to you?"*

* * * * * *

In the spring of 2013, Ron Coleman, along with his professional partner and wife Karen Taylor, traveled from their home on the remote Isle of Lewis off the coast of Scotland to Montgomery County, Pennsylvania, to give a two-day conference on hearing voices. I insisted that Annie accompany me, but she refused. She was a freshman in high school at that point, weaned off antipsychotic medication and holding her own in the Emotional Support program in high school. Her psychiatric diagnosis had changed to "recurrent clinical depression and OCD, with psychotic features." Since the sixth grade, Annie's voices had shown no signs of abating, and she still disliked talking about them or even acknowledging them. She told me many times she was embarrassed to have voices and did not want to advertise the fact. She also had no interest in learning anything *about* the voices. The single reason she finally agreed to go—and it would only be for the first day— was that it would be a day off from school.

As much as I wanted Annie with me at the conference, I was also nervous about it. I was not sure how receptive she would be to Ron's presentation, to his fresh-air views on a topic she preferred to keep tightly under wraps. It was mostly against her wishes, then, that we and approximately forty other voice hearers, support workers, mental health advocates, and family members assembled on a rainy spring morning to hear what this engaging Scotsman had to share.

Wearing a "Psychottish and Proud" T-shirt, Ron immediately captivated the audience with his disarming honesty and humor. *"How many voice hearers do we have in the room today?"* he asked. Ten to fifteen hands quickly shot up in the air. Annie's hand crept up. *"How many of you voice hearers right now hear your voices telling you to run out of this room as fast as you can?"* This time Annie raised her hand more swiftly, and we exchanged a knowing glance. Over the years, she had explained to me how threatened her voices felt by any direct confrontation, and for the first time, I thought about how stressed *the voices themselves* must be, trapped at the conference. With that one question, I could sense Annie pondering whether Ron might be a person who could truly understand her. *"How many of you voice hearers were ever asked by your psychiatrist what the voices actually say to you, besides 'are they commanding voices?'"* The same hands rose in the air, and so it went as Ron challenged one taboo after another around hearing voices. It was clear there would be no talk of auditory hallucinations that day, only invigoratingly candid discussion about life and the realities of hearing voices.

Ron admired voice hearers, respected the pathos of their lives and the strength of the human instinct that enabled them to survive trauma at any cost. He shared his own painful history of sexual abuse by a Catholic priest and the early suicide of his first love. He had spent a decade in and out of institutionalized care for schizophrenia, but, he said, he "gave up being schizophrenic" to work full-on toward recovery. He still hears voices but has learned to manage them, learns *from* them, and even thrives *with* them. Ron spoke of the many illustrious figures throughout history who heard voices, and he kept returning to the fact that hearing voices is, and always has been, part of the normal range of human experience. As a mental health trainer, consultant, advocate, and author, his mission, he said, was to educate the public about hearing voices and to empower voice hearers to live full and meaningful lives. I hoped Annie would take comfort not only from his encouraging message but from the knowledge that she was in good company with legions of others throughout the ages.

For Ron, recovery means the ability "to hold on to the self," both personally and in society. He believes that when the self is invalidated through destructive relationships, it struggles for composure and, if invalidated long enough and severely enough, it collapses, fragments, and becomes alienated from itself and from society. Another criterion of recovery for Ron is "wholeness," which for him means listening to all parts of ourselves. When we censor our emotions and suppress the strong feelings induced by trauma for too long, we lose the capacity to function well as human beings and members of society. We are missing actual pieces of ourselves, and, as a result, the internal structures break down. Ron traces the development of his voices in his book, *Recovery: An Alien Concept?*

Suppressing one's feelings is a normal coping strategy that many people employ to protect themselves from adverse life events. I suppressed my feelings for many years before I was forced to face them, and I now believe that the reason I heard voices was my refusal to explore and deal with my own distress. Though I was not prepared to examine what had happened in my life on a conscious level, this did not mean that my unconscious mind was doing the same. Indeed, much of the thinking around my voices is based on my belief that they appeared in order to alert me to the fact that my life was not whole. What I mean by that is that when we endure a major trauma (and refuse to deal with it) we cannot successfully suppress our emotions forever: there comes a point when they must be dealt with. Continual refusal to acknowledge even the existence of a problem brings with it the need to adopt ever more extreme coping mechanisms (in my case, self-isolation and playing sport in a violent manner that went beyond the norm of the game). Indeed, the fact that my voices started after an injury that ended my rugby career is indicative of the short-term usefulness of distraction-type coping strategies. Stripped of my means for dealing with my past forced my inner self into the position of reliving my expe-riences. However, my continual refusal to acknowledge the past traumas left my inner self with no option but to externalize them through the introduction of voices. I believe that it was my refusal to use the opportunity presented to me to explore the voices when they first started that caused me to be hospitalized. This refusal (like that of many others) is partly based on the societal belief that voices equate with insanity. This was the belief I held myself at the time, and the reality for me at that point was a simple one: I was mad. My secure self had vanished, to be replaced by a helpless and frightened self that felt controlled by the voices I heard.

* * * * * *

I returned for the second day of the hearing-voices conference without Annie because she made it clear that one day was all she would tolerate. Ron and Karen said the second day would be devoted to working with the voice hearers themselves, and everyone was invited to share in this experience. First, Ron had us separate into smaller groups comprised of mostly non-voice hearers around one voice hearer. The non-voice hearers in each group then asked the voice hearer questions and listened to what they shared. When we debriefed in the large group afterward, the common theme heard from our voice hearers was that of deep trauma and suppressed pain.

The premier event at the conference took place in the afternoon. On day one, Ron had selected a voice hearer from the audience who was willing to participate in a "voices pro-filing" exercise in front of the large group. "Brian" demon-strated no hesitancy coming forward. He had been taking antipsychotic medication for several years, with negligible improvement in his voices. Ron and Karen asked him a handful of simple questions, which helped them identify how many voices Brian heard, their gender, age, tone, and other general characteristics. As Brian spoke, Ron recorded his answers in graph form on a large pad and easel. On day two, Ron and Karen engaged Brian *and his voices* in a type of psychodrama. Brian seemed eager to continue the exercise. Seated in a semicircle, with one chair left vacant for the voices, Ron and Karen gently delved into the heart of Brian's personal story of trauma, delicately commenting on the events he shared and posing questions to both Brian and his voices. Brian related what his voices said to him, in the moment, word for word.

As Brian divulged his traumatic past, he became overwhelmed with emotion. Ron and Karen deftly unearthed layer upon layer of guilt he carried and then attempted to relieve him of that heavy load. Brian had been betrayed and abused by his father since he was a child, and through Ron and Karen's subtle intervention, he was able to access the innocent youngster who was taken advantage of and the vulnerable teenager who never had the chance to model himself after a respectable authority figure. It was breathtaking, heartrending theater, and at its conclusion, Brian's harshest voice, who represented his father, agreed to "go away" for two months, the amount of time Ron suggested. For the first time, Brian perceived a relationship between his voices and the traumas he had suffered, which seemed to him an astounding, energizing discovery.

Ron and Karen offered to further support Brian by helping him develop coping strategies to deal with the voices and invited him to stay at their Recovery House farm in Scotland. Voice hearers at Recovery House were given free accommodations and mental health support in exchange for doing chores around the Recovery House farm. Ron claimed that the most important job any voice hearer had at the Recovery House farm was to work on a recovery plan and get well, however long that took. Brian was not able to travel to Recovery House, but Ron and Karen planned to keep in touch with him through Skype to sustain the momentum of the work he had begun and provide a container for the raw emotions that had spilled out.

I felt sorry for the misfortune of Brian's early life and for the bleakness of his internal landscape. I wept and grieved for him, and then I did the same for my own daughter, glad now that she had not attended the second day of the conference to witness my despair. I knew I did not have the wherewithal to endure the voices as she did, but I wanted to project hope for her, so instead, I told her how awe-inspiring the day had been and how brave Brian was, both of which were true. Annie, too, had grit and was tougher and more resilient than I often gave her credit for, but I knew she would never expose her voices or traumas as fully as Brian had. I pretty much dragged her to that first day of the hearing voices conference, and there was no telling whether she would ever let her guard down again.

The following October, though, Ron and Karen returned, and to my great satisfaction, Annie attended both days of the conference. Ron went out of his way to take her aside and chat in private. She confided fragments of her second-grade experience with Sister Maria, and because of his own abuse at the hands of a respected Catholic priest, he was able to relate to her in a specific way. Later, as the three of us sat together, he asked Annie what she would ideally like to see happen with her voices, and she replied, *"At this point, I think I'll be living with them for the rest of my life, but I would like to not just exist with them. I'd like to have a really good life."*

Toward the end of the day, I had a chance to talk with Ron myself, and I asked him why years had elapsed between the advent of Annie's voices and the primary trauma of second grade. He explained there was often a cumulative pile-up of traumas before voices started. In Annie's case, he said, the last straw might have been the sixth-grade bullying.

* * * * * *

As a result of these two Ron Coleman conferences, Annie showed slightly more willingness to identify herself as a voice hearer and to consider what the voices said to her. Another excerpt from her writings around this time documents the beginning of her process of trying to make some sense of the voices:

Annie: I don't like to talk about the voices because it feels embarrassing to have them. They're too complex. I don't know why they do the things they do, but I guess it has something to do with all the guilt and shame I've felt since second grade. I can't piece it together like a puzzle. It's not clear-cut. It's not like I hear the actual voice of Sister Maria or someone else, the specific things they said; it just resembles them; it's more indirect and vague. The obsession that I had with the Devil and hell in second grade was behind everything. To have someone in that position [Sister Maria] tell you you're going to hell, hammering that into you, really does something to you ... saying you're a bad person if you don't go to church. She would not show any mercy and pounced on my vulnerabilities. There was so much unresolved trauma from that. I don't think trauma is ever really resolved. All those things stuck with me. When you're having all these emotions, intense emotions, it's like overload ... the voices are like a weird reaction to all the craziness you're feeling inside yourself.

Chapter 16

"When we acknowledge a child's feelings, we do him
a great service. We put him in touch with his inner
reality. And once he's clear about that reality, he
gathers the strength to begin to cope."

How to Talk so Kids Will Listen, Adele Faber and Elaine Mazlish

In between Ron and Karen's visits from Scotland, Annie's therapist Jean, who had also attended one of Ron's conferences, tried to pick up the threads of his work, but at that time, Annie mostly resisted her attempts. She preferred dealing with the "issue of the day," as Jean said, and often that issue was our latest blowup. Annie would pressure me to join her in the therapy room so we could rehash these arguments, but our sessions were so contentious Jean had to bring in a three-minute timer so I could finish a thought without a death stare and verbal trouncing from Annie. My presence in these sessions was, if anything, counterproductive to Annie's progress, but it was one way for her to obfuscate her deeper problems and avoid dealing with the voices.

There were some good things to come out of our time

together in therapy, though. Jean helped Annie construct a pictorial timeline of the emotionally charged events in her life, which represented a seismographic road map of her psyche. Some of the hot spots on that map seemed small in magnitude but revealing in their lasting impact. For instance, when she was still a child, and Mike and I were at our wit's end with her endless tantrums, he occasionally resorted to throwing out toys and once tossed her favorite stuffed animal, a purple unicorn my father had given her, in the garbage. This unhappy event appeared early and prominently on her timeline. Years later, Jean gave Annie a small metal unicorn she found at a yard sale, which Annie still displays on her dresser today, beside a vase of dried flowers. Other events on the timeline, such as second grade, the loss of Cara, and the bullying, were no surprise. This visual chronology gave Jean some overarching themes to work with. She was trained in hypnosis and EMDR therapy, a gentler type than I had experienced, but Annie was not an enthusiastic participant in the reprocessing technique or any other method that hovered too long over the nerve center of her pain. She was even more circumspect about her voices, but sometimes the submerged anguish came out sideways.

As with many teenagers, Annie hated any kind of rules or to hear the word "no." On one occasion, when I had denied what I considered an unreasonable request, she, as usual, refused to accept my answer, and I, in turn, refused to knuckle under. Once her anger erupted, there was no going back. She badgered me with increasing vehemence until, as usual, I withdrew emotionally and attempted to leave the room. Predictably, this enraged her, and she threw her body into the doorway in front of me, thrusting her arms in my chest, almost spitting at me as she shouted and screamed in my face. In desperation, I tackled her to the floor and, for a second or two, placed my hand over her mouth, not to hurt her but to stifle the verbal abuse. Now blind with fury, she fought me with all her strength, but I eventually overpowered her and ran from the house.

We spent the next several therapy sessions dissecting this event. Annie was incensed with me and rejected anything Jean or I said in my defense. I repeatedly apologized for putting my hand over her mouth, though qualifying each attempt with reasons why I was driven to it. Annie had a psychiatrist appointment directly following one of these bitter therapy sessions, and as we sat in the doctor's office for our quarter-hour visit, she was still seething, openly displaying her disgust with me. She practically begged the doctor to hospitalize her, but he was confused by her behavior and decided instead to increase her medication.

On the way home in the car, I told Annie I would agree to the hospitalization if she felt she needed it, and I apologized again for what I had done. I asked her what it was about *me* that so infuriated her, but she could not explain. I told her I really needed to know. She took a few deep breaths as she searched for an answer.

"It's not *you*," she said, "but you represent anyone who tries to overpower me." She told me she would never let what happened to her once happen again.

I asked her what she meant by that, and again she struggled to figure it out.

"The things that happened to me in sixth grade, with all the kids and the ...." She could not finish the sentence and seemed to be grappling with something else, fighting to stay with it.

"Did you feel like I was bullying you when I put my hand over your mouth?"

She was silent, still chasing the answer. "No," she said, *"but it's like ... like Sister Maria. I will never let that happen again!"* she cried out.

"What do you feel like she did to you?" I asked.

"I feel like she ... took away my voice. When you put your hand over my mouth, I felt like I was right back there with her, in second grade."

There it was, I thought, something I could understand and sympathize with. I thanked her for sharing such a painful insight.

✶ ✶ ✶ ✶ ✶ ✶

Annie's epiphany shook me. It was easy to forget what she had been through and how it still affected her. It was also easy to forget that the voices even existed. I knew they were always needling her, eroding her meager coping skills, but I could never ascertain what portion, if any, of her conduct was directly related to them. The voices had no bodily form, but their presence was as real to her as our dog Dexter and the two cats she doted on. She never visibly responded to them when she was with me, so I did not treat her any differently. The only clues were subtle and indistinct, a sudden flinching of her body, the times she asked what I had said when I had not said anything, or an abrupt, rather loud and melancholy "I Love You, Mom," which I intuited as a rebuttal to the voices' latest jab at me. I knew I was fair game for their shenanigans, especially considering our close, fraught relationship.

In later years, Annie told me that after our arguments, the voices toyed with her intense fear of death—*"Well, that's the last time you'll ever talk to her! This is how it ends. She's gonna die tonight! Where's your mom now—dead? You don't know what happens to her after death!"* Sometimes when I was not at home, she called me to see if I was still alive. I never doubted what she told me about the voices, never questioned their reality for her, never tried to tell her the voices were really "just your own thoughts." I accepted their reality from the start. Coexisting with the voices had become her way of being in the world, and if there was a way to make that more bearable, I wanted to help her find it.

Chapter 17

"Twenty years of medical research has shown that
childhood adversity gets under our skin, changing
people in ways that can endure in their bodies for
decades. It can tip a child's developmental trajectory
and affect physiology."

The Deepest Well, Nadine Burke Harris, MD

I first heard mention of a "Hearing Voices Movement" in 2011 when I read an article in *The Sun Magazine* titled "The Voices Inside their Heads," an interview with Gail Hornstein, Mount Holyoke College Professor of Psychology, by Tracy Frisch. Hornstein has been studying first-hand accounts of people with mental illness for decades and considers these individuals "experts of their own experience." In her book, *Agnes's Jacket: A Psychologist's Search for the Meanings of Madness,* she explores the topic of hearing voices in great depth. Like Ron Coleman, she believes that no person afflicted with mental illness is beyond hope, and she rejects the alienating medical language of the psychiatric community.

Hornstein explains that voices are not "'the inner speech'

most of us are familiar with, the internal monologue where we tell ourselves to do something or admonish ourselves." True voice hearing is something very different. Voice hearers, states Hornstein, "hear those voices through their ears, the way you are hearing my voice. Most people find it highly distressing. The experience often becomes overwhelming, especially if they don't tell anyone, which is common. Imagine if I started screaming obscenities at you and accusing you of things that only you would know you were potentially guilty of. It would be terrifying." According to Hornstein, the voices heard by voice hearers are as diverse as the people who hear them. Some sound like human voices, while others more resemble mumbling or static or animals or a machine or the maniacal laughter Annie often hears.

Hornstein's description of voices was remarkably close to Annie's day-to-day experience, and I was moved by her dedication to this unusual cause. I immediately ordered her book and sent a copy of The Sun article to our support team at Child and Family Focus. It was my first step out of the darkness surrounding hearing voices into the more enlightened, plain-speaking community of the "World Hearing Voices Movement."

For both Ron Coleman and Gail Hornstein, *disregarding the voices is not the answer*. Voices, they say, are more likely to get louder when ignored, and talking about what the voices say is one of the few things likely to diminish their intensity. Hornstein also attests that the reason people hear voices is that they have "experienced some kind of trauma that is too unbearable to remember directly." Victims are afraid to talk about the trauma and are therefore unable to work through their feelings about it. As a result, the psychological processing of the trauma breaks down, and the most harrowing, emotionally charged memories of the trauma go underground, remaining unintegrated and split off from the rest of the mind.

The processing of the traumatic episode is thus relegated to the unconscious, where it operates *autonomously*, "the way digestion does: we don't have control over it." For some individuals, the trauma eventually returns in the form of "voices."

I was fascinated by Hornstein's characterization of an autonomous, independent mechanism in the unconscious at the root of voices, and the phenomenon began to make a bizarre kind of sense. Like other defense mechanisms, they are mostly unconscious attempts to reduce anxiety by pushing back uncomfortable emotions, impulses, and thoughts. Most defense mechanisms are "primitive," the garden-variety type that originates in childhood, such as denial, regression, and projection. While defense mechanisms may help an individual deflect anxiety in the short term, the goal for human beings is to learn more mature ways to experience, accept, and cope with emotions as they get older.

Technically, hearing voices is considered one of the more sophisticated "dissociative" defense mechanisms. This category of defenses usually does not become activated until sometime past the early childhood years. Psychological dissociation is defined as "the splitting off of a group of mental processes from the main body of consciousness." These defense mechanisms manifest on a continuum, ranging from the mild detachment of daydreaming or "spacing out" from one's immediate surroundings to the more extreme states of amnesia, depersonalization (feeling detached from one's body and thoughts), and psychosis. While we can learn to become aware of the point at which we begin to use the simpler, more primitive defenses, the dissociative defense mechanisms steal over us and emanate from a more mysterious realm. Dissociative defense mechanisms separate individuals from their troubling memories and emotions in the real world. In cases of extreme trauma, they can be the most effective means of completely blocking out psychic pain; however, the achievement is attained at the steep price of severe psychological disturbance.

In slight contrast, Charles Fernyhough, Durham University psychology professor, sees a vital similarity between voice hearing and "inner speech." In his book *The Voices Within,* he posits that the inner dialogues we have, which are, again, a kind of splitting of the self and helpful in reasoning, can also be a safety mechanism in that they help channel inarticulate painful emotions into more comprehensible and digestible language. When people endure horrific ordeals, they frequently recall having automatically "dissociated" during the episode in order to survive the overwhelming stress—"Splitting itself into separate parts is one of the most powerful of the mind's defense mechanisms," states Fernyhough. These dissociated states can later take the form of voices, with a similar, creative point-counterpoint tone to ordinary inner speech, although with a more disturbed and negative quality.

Simon McCarthy-Jones, professor of clinical psychology and neuropsychology at Trinity College, proposes in his book, *Can't You Hear Them? The Science and Significance of Hearing Voices,* that hearing voices may "be driven by prior expectations" or "prior knowledge." Where science has traditionally viewed the brain as "passively drinking in signals from the external world" and then translating those signals into perceptual experiences, an alternative approach to understanding perception offers the "predictive processing framework." This theory contends that the brain automatically weighs any current actual sensory stimuli in its field against phenomena it has experienced in the past and calculates a "prediction error" for how accurately it will perceive the current stimuli. In other words, the brain "peeps at the past to predict the present," and then chooses, or predicts, the best hypothesis of reality based on the lowest prediction error. To some extent, then, the perceptions that register in the brain are more reflective of the brain's prediction of the experience than of the "actual thing 'out there.'" This process enables the brain to allocate a relatively small portion of its resources to dealing with the prediction error factor rather than wasting time and effort assessing every new sensory experience.

The therapeutic implication for voice hearers who hear distressing voices, according to McCarthy-Jones, is that to rid themselves of the voices, their brains "need to be persuaded that what [they are] experiencing is not best predicted as being a voice, but rather as being inner speech or a memory." One way to retrain the brain involves modifying the cues it takes in from the external world, which in turn colors its predictions of our perceptions. During and just prior to hearing voices, individuals often experience muscle tension and anxiety. If the body can be physically relaxed, say, through deep breathing, improved sleep, or medication, it might be possible to alter the cues which can trigger the dissociative mechanism of voices.

I could see where physiological adjustments might affect the environmental signals the brain relies upon. In times of greater stress, for instance, Annie's voices were usually at their worst, but if the brain were in the business of choosing the most apt perceptions, it seemed unfair that voice hearers, most of whom had traumatic backgrounds, had prediction errors unfairly weighted toward anguish and shame.

* * * * * *

The experience of hearing voices transcends purely biological, mechanistic explanations. As Daniel B. Smith writes of this enigma in *Muses, Madmen and Prophets:*

"[...] With voice hearing, all preliminary steps are by-passed. There is no breath, manipulation of air, no movement of bones or cochlea, not even a stimulation of the auditory nerve. With voice hearing, the brain, working alone in its watery chamber, creates a voice out of nothing but its own duplicitous silence. And it does so with such reality and finesse that the individual whose brain is engaging in such operations experiences the voice as if it were external. How is this possible? How can the brain create a voice in the absence of an external stimulus? How can the brain bypass the structures of the auditory system so successfully that it can produce not just sound but a voice, complete with modulation in pitch, tone, and volume, and with emotional tenacity? How can the brain transcend the external world?"

In other words, the modern psychiatric community is at a loss to explain voice hearing in any cause-and-effect, materialistic kind of way. The phenomenon of hearing voices, therefore, lends itself more to the language of metaphor. The neuroscientist Gerald Edelman compares the human brain to a jungle, with its countless tangled masses of neuronal networks. Spectacular feats of cooperation and connection occur among these jumbled neurons at every instant, enabling us to perform advanced neurological functions, but for the brain to operate optimally, he claims, it must deal with emotion. The brain's gears must be lubricated with the salubrious oils of unadulterated feelings. But as psychiatrist Mark Epstein writes, "Emotions are threatening. They move on nerve pathways that are faster than thought; they can take us by surprise and overwhelm our carefully constructed mental defenses. Emotions, by their very nature, are out of our control." This conception of the brain reminded me that the emotional fallout from Annie's second-grade trauma still lay buried in that dense jungle, dormant, menacing, but not likely to be fully uncovered. However, voices might emerge like vapors from that thick undergrowth, signaling where the embers of trauma still lay camouflaged.

However best we grasp the concept of voice hearing, according to people like Ron Coleman and Gail Hornstein, the only way voice hearers can come to grips with their voices is by venturing into the jungle itself. This means voice hearers must work on bringing to light, exploring, and even reliving events that might have engendered the voices. As they begin to reconstruct some of these distressing life experiences, voice hearers may find their voices possess a kind of contextual logic. They can be instructive, indicating the emotional issues voice hearers can least cope with and what they need help with. And, as Simon McCarthy-Jones discussed, if voice hearers can learn to retrain their brains by identifying the conditions, the bodily sensations, the thoughts and feelings that trigger an increase or change in the tone of their voices, they might find a way to manage their emotions, and possibly, by extension, their voices. Since we cannot tap directly into the brain's unconscious to figure out the mechanism that creates voices, we can at least approach it by re-creating the developmental stages that lead to their formation.

Chapter 18

> "At the very first meeting I attended, a group
> member asked me the question, 'Do you hear
> voices?' and when I replied that I did, responded
> with, 'They are real, you know.' This validation of
> my experience, as well as the validation of my 'self,'
> was a pivotal point in my recovery process."

Recovery: An Alien Concept? Ron Coleman

Gail Hornstein's article in *The Sun* also taught me about the crucial role of peer support groups for voice hearers. At that time, hearing voices support groups were spreading throughout Europe and slowly popping up in the United States. Ron Coleman talked about the importance of peer support groups at his conferences and recapped the oft-told story of how the very first group got started decades earlier by a Dutch psychiatrist named Marius Romme to help his suicidal patient, Patsy Hage. For their first year of therapy together, Romme viewed Patsy's voices through the conventional psychiatric lens, labeling them "hallucinations symptomatic of underlying psychosis." During one session, Patsy shouted at Romme,

"Why do you believe in a god you cannot see, but call the voices I hear every day unreal?" Patsy's question deeply affected Romme, and he began to wonder whether Patsy might feel better understood by another patient who heard voices. Soon he arranged for her to meet with two of his other voice-hearing patients and then observed them from the back of the room. Patsy, who had sat despondently with Romme for months, quickly perked up as the three women began sharing details of their experiences hearing voices. Romme was clearly on to something.

The support group principles, which worked so well for other populations, soon took hold within the hearing voices community. Dr. Sandra Escher, Marius Romme's professional partner and wife, explains that "even when someone is prepared to listen, the phenomenon [of hearing voices] is so extraordinary that it can be very difficult to convey to anyone entirely unfamiliar with such experiences. Mutual communication among voice hearers themselves is a practical solution to these problems"

According to Romme, voice hearers must first come to grips with the fact that they do indeed hear voices, the same way other people come to terms with different life challenges before they can develop effective strategies to deal with them. He adds, "The most difficult part of the voice hearing experience is feeling completely at the mercy of the voices, unable to affect or control them in any way." In their book, *Children Hearing Voices,* Romme and Escher talk about passive and active coping strategies for dealing with voices. Active coping strategies might involve listening to the voices only selectively; say, paying attention to the positive voices and ignoring the threatening ones, listening to them only at a certain time of day, joining a hearing voices support group, or keeping a diary of exactly what the voices say. They give examples in their book of creative ways they have witnessed children deal with voices, such as inventing video games that enable them to destroy the voices metaphorically. Active coping skills empower voice hearers to stand up to the voices and take charge of them, while passive coping strategies typically mean ignoring the voices, which may help in the short term but only perpetuate or exacerbate the problem in the long run.

* * * * * *

Annie was the first client our team at Child and Family Focus worked with who heard voices. However, the voices were rarely discussed; there were enough challenges to sort out already, and the two women were not conversant in "voices work." After reading the Hornstein article I sent them, though, they were interested to learn more and asked if there was any way they could help. I expressed my dream of finding a hearing-voices support group for Annie, and they once again sprang into action. A week later, they told me they had discovered a hearing-voices support group right in Montgomery County and then provided me with the name of the group facilitator, Berta Britz.

When we first contacted Berta, she explained that the support group she ran was not geared toward young people. She discouraged Annie's attendance because she thought she would find some of the voice hearers intimidating and hard to relate to. I was disappointed, but she quickly committed to helping Annie by creating a new, more age-appropriate hearing-voices support group. Child and Family Focus joined the cause by offering their spacious conference room as an inviting location for the group meetings. I could hardly believe this kind of support would soon be available, a mere two-minute car ride from my home.

It was months before the meetings got underway, but on that first evening, Berta waited for Annie at the conference room door with a warm smile. Water bottles, grapes, and cookies were neatly arranged for the guests on the side counter. Annie was the first to arrive and take a seat at the long conference table. I exchanged a few words with Berta and left, hoping Annie would be comfortable and that the group would go well. However, Annie told me later that no one else showed up that night. In fact, no one besides her showed up for the next several months. Berta and Annie were the group's only members, and even when Annie could not attend the meeting for some reason, Berta was there each week, snacks and all, on the chance that another young person in need of the same support might walk through the door. But gradually, through Berta's strenuous outreach efforts, the group attracted a modest gathering of young voice hearers searching for companionship, validation, and a safe place to share their common experiences.

A clinical social worker and voice hearer herself, Berta specialized in working with children and adolescents. Her association with the Hearing Voices Movement liberated her in a way she had not achieved before, and her deepest passion was helping young voice hearers "by creating spaces to welcome them as they grow into their fullest selves." Berta introduced the Hearing Voices Movement to our Pennsylvania community and was a founding member of the Montgomery County Hearing Voices Network. Like Ron Coleman, she transformed herself from a one-time psychiatric patient to an international speaker, trainer, consultant, and activist for the cause of hearing voices.

Berta connects to voice hearers through active listening; she insists that respect be given to whatever voice hearers reveal about their voices and to any personal meaning already attached to those voices. She explains to the group each week that the meeting is simply a time of sharing, not therapy or a replacement for medication. The only official stand the

Hearing Voices Movement takes on medication is that it should not be enforced. As I have often heard Ron Coleman say, the Movement is not against psychiatry—"only bad psychiatry." If members of the group find relief from medication, Berta urges them to stick with it.

Berta espouses the holistic approach of *creating a space* or a *"circle of trust"* to be fully and deeply heard. Writer and activist Parker Palmer writes, "A circle of trust is a group of people who know how to sit quietly 'in the woods' with each other and wait for the shy soul to show up. In such a space, we are freed to hear our own truth, touch what brings us joy, become self-critical about our faults, and take risky steps toward change—knowing that we will be accepted no matter what the outcome." For voice hearers in this supportive atmosphere, it may be a time to discover meanings inherent in their voices; for the circle of voice hearers together, it can be an opportunity to collaboratively explore interpretations and practice acceptance of each other. The group environment can also provide useful objectivity for voice hearers as they bounce off each other and gain more perspectives on their inner realities.

In addition to this search for meaning, Berta teaches voice hearers strategies to attain a more empowered relationship with their voices. She motivates voice hearers not to think of themselves as mentally ill or psychotic but rather as valuable human beings learning how to negotiate "the not uncommon phenomenon of voice hearing." Her approach, shaped by the Hearing Voices Movement, is to help voice hearers create a supportive social web, implement therapeutic strategies, and learn to respect different perspectives.

✳ ✳ ✳ ✳ ✳ ✳

Annie stayed with the group, on and off, for close to five years. As life changing as the support group was for her, it was also something of a mixed bag. Though Berta ensured that ground rules for confidentiality and safety were agreed upon at each meeting and provided members with plenty of space to share or vent, Annie sometimes felt there was too much free rein and legitimacy given to anything and everything the voice hearers said, including everything their voices said. She occasionally came home angry and frustrated by comments made at the meetings, and she sometimes felt that members fed off each other's voices, becoming more frenzied rather than more reasonable by the group dynamic. Some of her displeasure hit closer to home in that several members had voices immersed in far-fetched religious cosmologies, which disturbed her and added fuel to the fire she had been running from for years. Some nights members talked about anything *but* the voices, and once a group member was frighteningly intrusive in her personal life. But not least among the reasons she finally stopped going was the fact that she had always hoped to find a friend there, at least one other voice hearer whom she could relate to personally, which never happened.

*Annie: Some aspects of the support group were good. You can compare and contrast how your voices are versus someone else's. It's good to talk freely about them in a nonjudgmental way. It can clear up some things. The group helped me to co-exist with my voices. In some of the work I did with Berta and with Ron and Karen, I was able to realize that there's not too much truth or reality to what the voices say and that I can continue to live my life in spite of them. And if they say something like, I'm going to die if I don't do what they say, I know I'm not **really** going to die. I learned not to be so paranoid, to compartmentalize them more, tune them out. It's still scary and makes you anxious ... you still have the feelings of anxiety, like you're going to die if you don't do what* *the voices say, but there's some reality testing that's taken place.*

That peer support group, however, was the environment in which Annie learned to finally talk about her voices and begin to acknowledge them as parts of her own self. It was also how she came to understand and appreciate the common threads of our humanity, for she could see herself in the average non-voice-hearing individual as readily as she could in the most downtrodden voice hearer in any group. She had her favorite voice hearers over the years, young people I heard about whose innocence, earnest struggle, and spirit of good-will toward everyone in the group moved her. Despite her occasional complaints, for a long time, the group filled a deep need—she felt accepted, less alone, encouraged, supported, and listened to. It was validation of the most uncommon sort at just the right time in her life, and somewhere along the way, she developed a quiet determination to persevere and live as "normal" a life as anyone else.

Chapter 19

"Like other movements that seek to challenge
the authority of psychiatry's diagnostic categories,
the Hearing Voices Movement is controversial.
Critics point out that while depathologizing voice
hearing may feel liberating for some, it entails a risk
that people with serious mental illnesses will
not receive appropriate care."

"The Voices in our Heads," Dr. Jerome Groopman

Simon McCarthy-Jones has researched the origins of "voices" for two decades and states that the answer to this mystery has "profound implications for how we conceive of, and offer support for, voice hearing." In his book, *Can't You Hear Them? The Science and Significance of Voice Hearing,* he contends, "There is no need to advocate an either/or approach ... automatically reading autobiography into voices has the potential for harm. For example, you can imagine, and I have seen, someone hearing highly critical and abusive voices being put on the spot to answer questions as to why they 'really' hate themselves, even when they protest they don't. Some voices may be full of sound and fury but signify nothing about the person's past." In these situations, he claims, other, more biologically based explanations may be more appropriate. "Some people's voices may best be helped by a combination of psychiatrically delivered medication and a search for personal meaning in the voices; others may best be helped solely through medication, or solely through exploring and addressing the meaning of the voices. We have a vast array of expertise, and we need to know how and why to deploy it. [...] Yet there needs to be a more widespread engagement of psychiatry with the ideas of the HVM (Hearing Voices Movement)."

And what of the rare cases, less than 1 percent, where young children are diagnosed with schizophrenia? For several years, the story of Jani and Bodhi Schofield, now teenagers, was documented on the TLC tele-vision network. As with borderline personality disorder, diagnosing a child under twelve years of age with schizophrenia is devastating and controversial. In children that young, the symptoms of schizophrenia are also known to overlap with features of autism and "disruptive behavior disorders." However, both Jani and Bodhi exhibited portentous signs as far back as their parents, Susan and Michael, can remember, even as infants.

Bodhi and Jani suffered from severe agitation, engaged in self-harming behaviors, responded to an invisible world of visual and auditory hallucinations, and required regular hospitalizations. Susan and Michael reported that mental illness ran in both their families. Neither parent was ever accused of any type of neglect or abuse toward their children; rather, they worked tirelessly to keep them safe, extricate them from their enticing inner worlds, and to provide them with every therapeutic service available. Jani, the more verbal, outgoing older sister, started talking about her voices, visions, and invisible friends since she first began communicating, and her therapists were almost as familiar with them as they were with Jani. Bodhi was more inwardly imprisoned and prone to violent outbursts. Both children took an array of psychiatric medications, including antipsychotics. Jani has shown marked improvement in recent years, making friends at school, experiencing fewer voices and visions, learning life skills, and participating in more mainstream classes and outside activities. Though Bodhi has been slower to improve, both parents remained hopeful.

To suggest that psychosocial trauma lay at the root of Jani and Bodhi's difficulties would be unthinkable to me.

* * * * * *

Critics of the Hearing Voices Movement argue that its individualized approach to voice hearing weakens psychiatry's authority. They caution that voice hearers considered too mentally ill to take on their voices will only get worse because they will be encouraged to forgo medication. This misinterpretation of the HVM's stand is prevalent even among members of the family support group I attended. At one meeting, a family member respectfully admitted that he felt his son, in his early 20s, had been more hurt than helped by his peer support group experience because it had unrealistically increased his son's confidence in recovering without medication. This, in turn, increased his reluctance to seek further treatment, sending him into another psychiatric crisis.

In response to this father's legitimate concern, another parent in our group described his own experience of attending a peer support meeting for his daughter. Although non-voice hearers are barred from these meetings, the facilitator made an exception in his case because of the long distance he had traveled to determine whether the group would be beneficial for his daughter. He reported that at his meeting, voice hearers discussed the medications they took and encouraged each other to continue with them if they felt even a minimal stabilizing effect. He also observed members sharing strategies to manage the voices, and he was impressed by the overall atmosphere of acceptance and camaraderie.

The Hearing Voices Movement advocates for the right of voice hearers, either alone or in collaboration with family, friends, therapists, and psychiatrists, to make their own decisions regarding medication. I sympathize with the gravity of the choice at hand. The adverse long-term effects of certain psychiatric medications are enough to deter anyone from taking them unless they are absolutely necessary. The side effects can far outweigh the benefits, and the hazards of withdrawal are also alarming. When Annie was twenty-one and attempting to withdraw from medications that again were not helping her, she was given no clear instructions by her psychiatrist on how to safely taper off, and the medical emergency that ensued nearly landed her in the hospital.

Despite how ardently I support the Hearing Voices Movement, I confess to having been a reticent participant in our family support group meetings, reluctant to pontificate too passionately on its virtues. The group was originally formed as a service to "allies" of voice hearers, those individuals who are uncertain where to turn and in need of encouragement when they discover their loved ones troubled by hearing voices. Although the list of group members grew quickly, the message of the Movement was slow to penetrate. The experience of hearing voices is what attracts new members, but the shift toward endorsing a more holistic treatment model can be difficult to fully embrace in the face of desperate psychiatric crises. When one of our loved ones was in jail or held up in the courts or refusing to leave the house or rejecting any form of treatment, we all felt the helplessness. When we occasionally heard about an aggressive episode by a loved one, compassion was complicated by concern for personal safety, and the promise of the Hearing Voices Movement seemed inadequate and simplistic. But it is the most welcoming and humane of starting points, and its fundamental objective is worth fighting for—"to envisage and enact a society that understands and respects voice hearing, supports the needs of individuals who hear voices, and values them as full citizens" (Longden).

✳ ✳ ✳ ✳ ✳ ✳

Our support group meetings were held at a Quaker Meeting House, a venerable gathering place beating with the heart of Quaker compassion and tolerance. In his book *A Quiet Haven: Quakers, Moral Treatment, and Asylum Reform,* Professor Charles Cherry writes that for centuries Quakers have believed that "even the most severely afflicted of the mentally ill retain that spark of the Light which makes them God's children and part of a religious community." Quakers were sensitized early on to the plight of those troubled in mind, partly because their own focus on eliciting a direct experience of God rather than appealing to external religious authority stigmatized them as "mad" religious enthusiasts. Their renowned "Moral Treatment" of the "distracted" melded compassionate care with abundant personalized attention and practical therapeutic prescriptions. Where one person might benefit from an emphasis on intellectual diversion, another individual's emotional faculties might be stirred by religious worship, and still another might best find solace and strength through regular manual labor.

The Quakers' famous "Retreat," established in York, England, in 1796, was the first institution to house and treat the mentally ill in a humane and dignified way. The Moral Treatment included "walks and farm laboring in pleasant and quiet surroundings. There was a social environment where residents were seen as part of a large family-like unit built on kindness, moderation, order, and trust. There was a religious dimension, including prayer. Inmates were accepted as potentially rational beings, who could recover proper social conduct through self-restraint and moral strength. They were permitted to wear their own clothing and encouraged to engage in handicrafts, to write, and to read books. They were allowed to wander freely around The Retreat's courtyards and gardens, which were stocked with various small domestic animals" ("Quakers in the World").

The Moral Treatment was extolled in its day because it was effective where other approaches failed. Its success had the power to rewrite the prevailing biologic theory of mental illness, which led to fundamental legal reform and overall improvements in care. In the United States, however, persons with mental illness were locked away in large, impersonal, often prison-like asylums, where harsh, inhumane treatments were frequently used. The cruelties conducted within these institutions persisted until the journalistic advocacy work of people like Dorothy Dix and Nellie Bly in the 1800s and early 1900s began to slowly nudge the pendulum back toward more compassionate care.

In the early 1900s, psychoanalytic therapies, "talking cures," were instituted, but uncovering unconscious motives for behavior is a lengthy process dependent upon the right therapeutic rapport and not conducive to the rigors and cost of institutional care. More expedient, magic-bullet interventions were sought by the 1940s and 1950s, as chemists began experimenting with different ingredients that could provide relief to mentally ill patients by calming imbalances in the brain to achieve some facsimile of serenity and balance.

Some of the medications worked, like lithium for bipolar disorder, and by the late 1950s, the decision was made to begin migrating the enormous number of institutionalized patients out into the communities, armed with little more than prescription medications. Communities were slow to adapt to the needs of this onslaught and offered virtually no assistance with housing, job training, counseling, or practical life skills. Eventually, for many of these individuals, helplessness and the lack of opportunity led to a relapse in symptoms, homelessness, drug use, criminal behavior, or incarceration. As destructive and chaotic as this was, the deinstitutionalization of patients was the rudimentary precursor to the reform we sometimes see today, where community agencies, consisting of mental health counselors, social workers, and the like, partner with struggling individuals to provide the help they need without entering psychiatric facilities. Child and Family Focus, the agency our family worked with, once described its goal as empowering Annie to manage and thrive "in the least restrictive environment possible."

* * * * * *

The spirit of the Quaker Moral Treatment is alive in today's Hearing Voices Movement, the York Retreat reminiscent of Ron Coleman's Recovery House Farm. Annie was once invited by Ron to spend time at Recovery House during her summer break. I, too, was invited because of her young age, but it was too drastic a measure for her. She had no desire to participate in farm life, and she was intimidated by the total commitment required. Though that dream never became a reality, it was curative just to know that Recovery House existed.

Recovery—the belief that voice hearers are entitled to and capable of leading productive, satisfying lives—is the clarion call of the Hearing Voices Movement. Recovery does not necessarily mean the voices cease to exist, according to the HVM, but rather that the individual has been restored to a healthy, purposeful life.

The original mental health recovery movement was influenced by the first activist groups, which formed in the 1960s and 1970s. These groups were comprised of former patients whose shared experiences of disturbing encounters with mental health professionals motivated them to create their own grassroots networks of support. The recovery movement rejected psychiatry's emphasis on symptoms and diagnoses, as well as the power differentials existing between mental health professionals and patients. It gradually inspired positive change, most notably in the form of "patient-centered care," more holistic services, and less stigmatizing language. The objective of patient-centered care is to empower individuals to formulate their own goals based on personal values and needs and to guarantee an active role in the choice of treatments through a shared decision-making process with a team of mental health care providers.

The goal of today's more progressive factions of the mental health recovery movement is to place individuals with lived experience at the helm of mental health care reform, allowing them "to reclaim the definition, process, and experience of recovery as their own" (Hunt, Resnick). Implicit in this message is the fact that individuals who happen to hear voices are as valuable as all other human beings and entitled to the same right to determine their own lives.

Chapter 20

"It is to our detriment that we live in a culture that
does not honor the internal world. In many cultures,
the internal world of dreams, feelings, images,
and sensations is sacred."

Waking the Tiger: Healing Trauma, Peter A. Levine

In the mental health field, much is made of a symptom called "anosognosia," a Greek word meaning "to not know a disease." Individuals with anosognosia are unable to distinguish their "psychotic" symptoms from "consensus reality," a term Paris Williams uses in his book *Rethinking Madness* to refer to the "agreed upon set of beliefs and experiences within an individual's culture which are considered valid and the basis of 'reality.'"

Anosognosia occurs in about 50 percent of individuals diagnosed with schizophrenia and in about 40 percent of those with bipolar disorder. It prevents individuals from gaining a full understanding of their condition and creates a major obstacle to psychiatric treatment. Anosognosia also disrupts personal relationships and interferes with one's ability to function in society. Because persistent untreated psychotic symptoms have the potential to shift the mind further and further from consensus reality, anosognosia can set a person adrift in that remote sea until the coastlines of sanity gradually fade from view. "Poor insight" in psychiatric patients is considered, by turn, the result of ordinary, powerful denial, the product of acute psychological defensiveness, or even the consequence of a dysfunction in the brain's frontal lobe. Anosognosia or not, the Hearing Voices Movement argues that the wiser course is not to try to convince voice hearers that their voices are not real. They *are* real to the voice hearer; in fact, as one voice hearer states, they are "even more real in the way they boom out at me from both inside and outside."

Annie was only too aware of the dichotomy between her everyday consensus reality and the landscape of her anomalous experiences. Her voices are not the "hidden alters" of dissociative identity disorder. They are not separate identities that animate her. They may represent parts of her personality, but they are not *actual* personalities living independent lives. When we interact with Annie, we know exactly who she is; her essence is always the same.

In addition to the voices, Annie negotiated "visions"— fleeting, frequently gory glimpses of carnage and destruction she was too ashamed to reveal in detail. The visions, she told me, were unnerving and painted the world in depressingly lurid brushstrokes. Nighttime dreams were also gruesome. Sometimes when she described the torments of her latest nightmare, it was as if she just managed to make it back alive from the lowest circle of hell. As she got older, she tried different, stronger sleep medications, again with only minimal success. There were times when Annie wanted to know exactly what was wrong with her, why she experienced all the hideous things she did, but as her therapist, Jean, said, "What would be the benefit of a label?" Her condition defied easy categorization, and to me, her lack of anosognosia tethered her to the here-and-now, allowing us to maintain a sense of normalcy and the hope that better days might lie ahead. Self-awareness and the capacity for insight have also enabled her to keep a grasp on consensus reality, keep her voices and visions from overwhelming her, and keep her head above the threatening waters of anosognosia.

But according to Dr. Bessel van der Kolk, professor of psychiatry at Boston University School of Medicine and noted expert on trauma, the capacity for insight and the willingness to undergo therapy may not be enough to help a traumatized individual. Trauma "lodges" in the body, he claims, and any effective psychiatric treatment presents special challenges because it needs to engage the whole person. In his book, *The Body Keeps the Score: Brain, Mind and Body in the Treatment of Trauma*, he writes:

"For a hundred years or more, every textbook of psychology and psychotherapy has advised that some method of talking about distressing feelings can resolve them. However, the experience of trauma itself gets in the way of being able to do that. No matter how much insight and understanding we develop, the rational brain is basically impotent to talk the emotional brain out of its own reality. I am continually impressed by how difficult it is for people who have gone through the unspeakable to convey the essence of their experience. It is so much easier for them to talk about what has been done to them—to tell a story of victimization and revenge—than to notice, feel, and put into words the reality of their internal experience. [...] Being traumatized means continuing to organize your life as if the trauma were still going on—unchanged and immutable—as every new encounter or event is contaminated by the past. After trauma, the world is experienced with a different nervous system. The survi-

vor's energy now becomes focused on suppressing inner chaos at the expense of spontaneous involvement in their life. These attempts to maintain control over unbearable physiological reactions can result in a whole range of physical symptoms."

Some of the treatments Dr. van der Kolk employs include psychodrama, yoga, neurofeedback, EMDR, and various kinds of play.

* * * * * *

Another diagnosis Annie regularly received over the years is "Post-Traumatic Stress Disorder" (PTSD), which was something of a catch-all, responsible for triggering everything from her OCD to her voices. No defense mechanism seems formidable enough to deter PTSD's powerful flashbacks, nightmares, and intrusive memories brought on by past trauma. In his book *Waking the Tiger,* Dr. Peter Levine sees post-traumatic stress disorder not as an illness to be managed but as the result of the natural process of healing gone awry. Like Bessel van der Kolk, he states, "Most trauma therapies address the mind through talk and the molecules of the mind with drugs. Both of these approaches can be of use. However, trauma is not, will not, and can never be fully healed until we also address the essential role played by the body." The body responds to trauma in a profound way, according to Levine: It "tenses in readiness, braces in fear, and freezes and collapses in helpless terror." The body is designed to normalize itself after trauma, but if that intuitive process does not complete itself for any reason, undue suffering is in store for the individual. We can be healed from trauma, Levine assures us, even spiritually awakened and transformed by it, if we have the proper guidance, receive enough social support, and learn how to reconnect with our natural biologic instincts.

Levine has been "working to untangle the vast mysteries of trauma" for three decades and believes trauma is intricately related to the physical and natural sciences. He contends that we have much to learn from animals in the wild because they "exemplify nature in balance" and provide "insight into the biological healing process." Like animals, when human beings confront overwhelming threats to their safety, the instinctual, primitive part of the nervous system kicks in, enabling them to move through the crisis in any of three ways: by fighting back, by fleeing, or by shutting down, or "freezing." This third option is activated only when the first two are obstructed or when we become so paralyzed with fear that the body constricts with pent-up emotion, immobilizes, and literally freezes (Annie in second grade). The freezing response is nature's last resort at protection and propels us into maximum defensive mode to anesthetize us against the impending disaster. However, where animals eventually pass through the freezing stage and shake off the frustrated physiological impulses, PTSD sufferers get stuck there. The anxiety produced by the trauma never dissipates.

The symptoms of PTSD, according to Levine, represent *energy*—specifically, the residual energy once mobilized by the body to surmount the original danger. That concentration of trapped energy is like an "indestructible time bomb," liable to go off under any number of circumstances. He believes that at some point, it needs to be discharged from the body if we are to recover our lost selves. The key to healing from traumatic events, for Levine, lies in our ability to "mirror the fluid adaptation" of animals as they pass through the freezing response, shake out and release the trapped energy, and regain their former strength and vitality.

Tapping into the physiological cycle of trauma and reconnecting with frightening sensations and emotions is a challenge for PTSD sufferers, but Levine says this process does not necessarily mean reliving the original trauma or dredging up its charged memories. He provides exercises in his book to help traumatized individuals gently enter a mild state of trauma by slowly eliciting the arousal cycle. If we can attune ourselves to these bodily sensations without interpreting them or trying to change them, he claims we can learn to consciously utilize them to our benefit, even years or decades after the trauma occurred.

There is a basic biological rhythm to trauma, Levine attests. If we become receptive and patient enough to observe the sensations, images, and thoughts that arise in these aroused physiological states, we can watch them ebb and flow and gradually transform into other thoughts, sensations, and images until they gently diminish. In this final stage, we can flow through the fear and become unstuck. This phase is almost always accompanied by physical trembling, vibrations, shaking, sobbing, waves of warmth, and other kinds of relaxation of the muscles, which eventually resolve in a deep feeling of calm, denoting safety, comfort, and peace.

* * * * * *

Occasionally someone suggests that Annie's voices might be a sign of psychic giftedness, that if she could learn to turn down the volume on the mean-spirited voices, she would better discern the more benevolent ones, which might hold spiritually significant messages. Of course, she would also need to learn how to sweep the psychic path clear of negativity—through meditation, visualization, rituals, mindfulness, and prayer—to protect herself from the darker energies swirling in her mind's vortex and tune in to this spiritual channel.

This concept puts me in mind of shamans, practitioners of psychic healing who intervene for individuals by accessing the spirit world. From the shamanistic perspective, the trapped energy of a person's trauma is considered "displaced," an "intrusion." Like van der Kolk and Levine, shamans also view the displaced energy as the residuum of strong unexpressed emotions stored in the body, where it interferes with the flow of psychic currents. They do not view the energy as inherently good or bad, but as simply misplaced and therefore having the potential to cause harm. The shaman's purpose is to "extract" the misplaced energy and restore the individual's integrity and balance.

Shamans first undergo their own painful experiences, excruciating visionary journeys which initiate them into the inner workings of the mind and soul and connect them on a profound level with the elemental forces of nature. They work their "magic" in ritualized ceremonies using dance, music, drumming, chanting, whatever works to achieve a trance-like state of consciousness—"soul flight"—which allows them to "see" into the body's energy patterns and locate the source of the individual's displaced energy. The shaman communicates with other healing spirits while in the soul flight to help determine and address the specific cause of the individual's problem and to gain more power to heal. The shaman then removes and discards the misplaced energy, thereby freeing the individual of its psychic obstruction. The discarded energy is ideally transmuted by the shaman into more life-enhancing energy and then poured into the void left by the extraction.

Annie and I once watched a movie about an African voice hearer who underwent shamanic healing. The woman's psychological crisis spanned several years, and in the end, the outcome was so positive that whether she still heard voices was irrelevant. She had reconciled with her family and children, come to terms with severe childhood trauma, re-engaged with society, and was now helping others through their own spiritual crises.

Shamanic healing sounded exotic and wonderful; in fact, I was ready to cart Annie off to the nearest shaman—if only I could find one.

* * * * * *

Some voice hearers experience psychosis as part of what is called a psychospiritual crisis or "spiritual emergency," which can be prompted by a wide variety of physical or emotional causes. Psychotherapist Christina Grof and her husband and psychiatrist Stanilov Grof coined the term spiritual emergency to convey both the sudden appearance of the crisis and the emerging opportunity to ascend to a higher level of spiritual awareness and psychological health. According to the Grofs, many of the conditions diagnosed as psychosis are not "manifestations of an unknown pathological process" but the "result of a spontaneous movement in the psyche that engages deep dynamics of the unconscious and has healing and transformative potential." Clinically, the stages of the process can resemble psychosis, but rather than indiscriminately suppress the condition with medication, the Grofs profess that if given the proper understanding and guidance, individuals can navigate through the psychospiritual crisis and emerge emotionally healed and spiritually evolved.

The Grofs believe the common denominator of these situations involves a "radical shift in the balance between unconscious and conscious processes," brought about by individuals' psychological turning inward as they become engrossed in the crisis. This mental absorption can eventually induce a weakening of psychological defenses and an increase in the energy charge of the psyche's unconscious material, which can then emerge into consciousness. Many of the psychospiritual emergencies the Grofs have identified have overlapping qualities, but there are enough defining characteristics to differentiate them. The Grofs explore, for example, the shamanic crisis, awakening of Kundalini, episodes of unitive consciousness, near-death experiences, past-life experiences, psychological renewal through a return to the center, communication with spirit guides, channeling, and other crises of "psychic opening."

The Grofs acknowledge that the modern-day psychiatric community still pathologizes these mystical states. Psychospiritual crises can have blurry boundaries, though, and the Grofs caution that close monitoring is crucial because "there also exists the opposite error of romanticizing and glorifying psychotic states or, even worse, overlooking a serious medical problem." And as Lionel Corbett, Professor of Depth Psychology, states in his book, *The Religious Function of the Psyche,* "Although the experience of the autonomous psyche can be deeply healing, in fragile personalities it can trigger severe disorganization."

* * * * * *

Annie has often told me she feels connected to "another world" somehow, but she does not think she is destined to become a spirit-channeling medium. When I ask whether she feels her voices are in any way related to this psychic potential, she says she does not believe that the reason her mind is filled with so much negativity is because she has a psychic gift. She hypothesizes, though, that her extreme emotional sensitivity might have left her susceptible to both negative and positive aspects of mental health, to both voices and a psychic sensibility. She feels deeply what others feel and says she sometimes "anticipates" events that later occur. Occasionally she listens to real-life conversations around her (not the voices) with the conviction that she has heard them before, each word, each phrase, and each sentence. She also sometimes feels that she knows what people are going to say before they even open their mouths.

Annie decided to visit a spiritual medium when she was twenty-five years old, hoping for a tonic to her ongoing preoccupation with death. She had always felt deeply connected to those family members who died, even those whom she had never met, like my mother and Billy, and she hungered for validation that they were together and content in the afterlife. She was especially close to my father, but as his health failed and her troubles worsened, his weekly visits from Brooklyn gradually ceased. When he died at the age of eighty-eight, she was only thirteen and had just returned from the group home. She could not bring herself to say goodbye to him in the hospital, not only because she could not bear to see him so close to death, but because she felt he would be disappointed in her. She worried that he had held that choice not to visit him against her and still felt guilty about it.

Although the medium gave her mild comfort of the sort she needed, the most compelling part of her "reading" was the message that Annie herself seemed to have the same psychic abilities she did. She encouraged Annie to develop and harness this faculty, which would help transform the consternation in her mind into a gift. Furthermore, she said, Annie's dead ancestors were her psychic guides, and it made sense that she so strongly embraced them.

Annie had this to say about the experience:

Annie: *"You know, what's interesting about you, Annie, is that I'm picking up a very strong, familiar energy. I think you're like me." I could guess what the medium was alluding to, it being a thought I had frequently pondered myself since childhood. Between vivid dreams that prematurely imitated life, distinct premonitions of significant changes to come, and a profound feeling of connection* *to my loved ones on the other side despite never even having met some of them, my gut had long ago signaled mediumship as a possibility.*

In my younger years, this was a fact I had believed to be certain. Often, I expressed to my mother, "I can't explain it, but I know something is there. There is just too much evidence," grappling to articulate to her the recurring psychic incidents I continued to encounter. Sometimes a believer in this kind of spirituality herself, as well as even being told later in life that she, too, had a gift, my mother never denied my ability. In fact, she sincerely validated it, never once scoffing or making me feel crazy.

It was not until I understood that such occurrences were generally rejected by society that I began to suppress my intuitiveness, doubting its validity altogether. I observed how the psychiatrists looked at me as I attempted to explain the voices and visions I experienced, the grim concern in their eyes. If I was being told that these visions were not "real" but instead indicators of serious mental illness, how could my clairvoyance be any different? I no longer spoke about the feelings of connection to something otherworldly and shoved it down, taking a page out of what I had learned while navigating the mental health system for so many years—it was better to not talk at all than to say too much. A string of coincidences, that's all it was, I dejectedly concluded.

In hindsight, I believe that the effects of my intuitive neglect were grave. I was no longer confident about what awaited me in the afterlife. Now it was the unknown that flipped my entire existence upside down. The childlike belief that there was no question of another place after this one was gone, and I struggled greatly to think about anything other than an eternity of separation between my loved ones and me. There was an immense feeling of shame for ever having considered that I had a gift or could be "special." But most of all, I lost the powerful, internal compass that I had trusted for guidance, the tool that pointed me in the direction I needed to go. Without this compass, many dark days were in store for me.

"Have you ever thought this about yourself?" the medium inquired during our session. I hesitated, nodding. "I don't want to sound stupid, but I have. I've wondered this since I was a little girl. I've had a number of psychic happenings." A wide smile spread across her face, and she clapped her hands together, exclaiming, "I knew it! I knew it the second we began; I knew you were like me. Oh, I'm so happy! Welcome to the other side. A baby medium has been born." I laughed, wiping tears from my eyes, grateful beyond comprehension for the long-awaited words of validation I had just received. "Embracing your powers is going to be your key to the life you are meant to live," she finished. "You have a gift."

Maybe I wasn't a complete lunatic, maybe there was hope after all, I reflected after we had finished our session. For the first time in a long time, I exhaled.

❄ ❄ ❄ ❄ ❄ ❄

It would be difficult to view Annie's voices exclusively through the rosy lens of incipient psychic abilities or the lofty purposefulness of spiritual emergencies. And shamanistic healing sounds beguiling but also grander and more optimistic than either of us would dream possible. However, the human psyche has inexhaustible potential for healing. Aspects of these approaches could help burnish the blunt instruments of clinical psychiatry, take some of the sting out of a severe mental illness diagnosis, and provide a beacon of unconventional hope to the suffering.

Chapter 21

"First, I was in consistent talk therapy, with a psychoanalyst who understood me and treated me with respect. With his painstaking interpretations of my behaviors, White helped me open a window onto myself, showing me that my psychosis served to protect me from painful thoughts and feelings. My psychosis actually played a role in my psychological life—the unconscious mind serving as a defender of the conscious mind. For some reason, knowing that made everything less toxic, more malleable. I may not have been in complete control of my psychosis, but I wasn't totally at its mercy, either. In addition, White did not recoil from me. He never put me in the hospital (under the guise of protecting me while actually protecting himself), but stood his ground when I was most frightening, and vowed to protect me. He knew better than anyone most of the time, I was literally scared out of my wits."

The Center Cannot Hold, Elyn Saks

Elyn Saks, Professor of Law, Psychology, and Psychiatry at the University of Southern California Law School, writes about her struggles with schizophrenia in *The Center Cannot Hold: My Journey through Madness*. She manages her illness, characterized by chaotic, disorganized thinking, mood difficulties, and the inability to distinguish reality from psychosis, through a balancing act of strong medication, intensive therapy, and the consistent love and support of her husband, friends, and family. With the right resources, she says, "we who struggle with mental illness can lead full, happy, productive lives."

Saks maintains that years of psychoanalytic treatment were indispensable in her recovery. In a recent interview, she explained that "a lot of therapists have a rule where their patients cannot articulate their delusions or hallucinations—but to me you need to have a place where you can do that, where it's safe. It's sort of like a steam valve." She believes that her psychotic symptoms are not just "the random firing of neurons that don't have any meaning," but that they "tell you some truth about your psychological reality." For example, if a delusion or hallucination tells her that she's killed people, "it's really an archaic way of saying I feel like a very bad person." She admits, however, that even if we make meaning of symptoms in this way, our interpretation usually does not help at the time we experience them. For that reason, she contends, we need to strengthen the "observing ego," a process akin to mindfulness, in which we mentally step back and observe our thoughts and feelings without getting swept up in them. This practice allows Saks to gradually detach from the delusion or hallucination and say to herself, "Oh, Elyn, that's just your illness acting up. Pay it no mind."

Annie articulates how challenging it is and how dubious the payoff can be to find meaning in her voices. Her observing ego, although functioning, could use strengthening to stave off the anxiety, but the hard-wiring she talks about here is the nonnegotiable essence she struggles with:

> **Annie:** *A lot of the most triggering things for the voices are related to religion and death, Sister Maria, all the guilt, the idea that I'm a bad person, the fear that I'm going to hell, all the uncertainties surrounding death. The voices are almost always negative; they're random, and you can't make sense of the commentary. Once in a while,*

there are connections that are clear, and sometimes I can tell it's my anxiety at work. It's like there's just so much anxiety in me that it switches over to voices; it bubbles over to the voices. I don't think it really changes anything to realize the connections voices have to real life. I think there's too much focus on that. It's good to know, yeah, but it doesn't change anything for me. Sometimes, a lot of times, the voices aren't the worst things— it's more the anxiety. My anxiety bothers me sometimes more than the voices, and then the anxiety drives the voices. I was always just so tuned in to everything around me ... Joe's friends made me feel anxious if they weren't nice to this one or that one, the boy in my class sitting by himself made me feel anxious because I thought he was lonely or might feel bad ... I just couldn't stand anyone being mean to people, and I would feel it if they were. I just really feel things deeply; I'm hard-wired that way.

* * * * * *

In *The Quiet Room*, Lori's psychiatrist speaks about the primitive fear we have that our thoughts have power and how it is "one of the reasons some cultures have superstitions about saying things out loud." When Lori was angry with her father, for instance, her psychiatrist reminded her that anger was a normal feeling, that there was nothing bizarre or unexpected about that feeling. But when, as often happens with human beings, Lori's feelings slowly turned into fantasies, and then into fantasies of the horrible disasters we sometimes imagine as the climactic result of our fears, she began to believe she was creating those disasters. "Locked away in her own world, Lori just didn't have any way of putting her thoughts and emotions into perspective." As her psychiatrist told Lori, "You have to remember that it's normal to feel angry, but that your thoughts can't harm anyone. You don't have that power, but you do have the power to influence the direction of your thoughts."

Both Elyn and Lori denied their illness for years as their lives deteriorated, but eventually, they engaged with empathetic professionals who were not constrained by standard psychiatric practices. These workers met Elyn and Lori in the reality of their psychoses and interacted with them as complex human beings capable of getting better and moving on with their lives. They were not afraid to call forth the voices and meet them on their own terms. They treated the whole person; they were therapists, psychiatrists, and spiritual counselors all wrapped up in one. They were part of the psychiatric establishment, and they also encompassed the ethos of the Hearing Voices Movement.

Chapter 22

> "To some degree, the brilliant façade of a good face
> and a good outfit protects me. My sickness is rarely
> obvious. I don't have to tell new people in my life
> about it. Although I no longer fret about when to
> disclose my psychiatric condition, I'm still aware of
> the shift that occurs when it happens."
>
> *The Collected Schizophrenias, Esme Weijun Wang*

In *The Voice Inside,* Paul Baker states, "Those people we know who are recovered all learned to express themselves, to give up shame and guilt after learning to manage their anxiety about their voices. They often wrote their stories down and then learned to talk about what has happened. Some people have even started to speak in public and discovered that they have had useful experiences that they can share with others." But he also comments on how easy it can be to "underestimate the great difficulty people find in talking about the original problem that led to the voices." Many victims of abuse, for example, have been so intimidated by their voices that telling the full story goes against every instinct. These voice hearers might fear harm will come to their loved ones or that the voices will torment them more than ever by going public.

Occasionally, Annie is asked to speak at a mental health event on the effect of trauma in her life, but when she conjures up that time of Sister Maria, she will only hint at it. She keeps the contours and magnitude of her suffering off limits and the disquieting memories firmly tucked away. She does not think anyone can really understand or identify with it and does not want to risk the further disappointment and shame of being misunderstood.

I have often wondered over the years how understanding someone would be upon learning that Annie hears voices all day, every day. Does she feel a need, though, to tell an intimate other about the voices, or for that matter, does she feel compelled to tell *anyone* about her voices? The answer, she says, is no. She does not feel a pressing need to tell anyone about her voices, but there is a definite drawback. An essential part of her remains unknowable to others, and that gap in knowledge is impossible to bridge. She does not necessarily need it bridged, she says, but she would occasionally like to meet someone halfway, be able to discuss difficult topics like voices, and have a relationship defined by openness and mutual support.

Annie has a recurring dream, a "horrific, bloody," dream, in which she is paralyzed and tries to scream, but nothing comes out of her mouth. One late summer afternoon, as we sit on the back-porch unwinding after our workdays, she tells me that she had the dream again the previous night and describes it in more detail. I do a quick online search on my laptop and read her a bit of the dime-store psychology on Google. In the world of dreams, it seems, when a person tries to scream or yell, but no sound comes out, a powerful emotion is trying to express itself. The individual is having difficulty communicating that emotion and is angry and frustrated that no matter how hard she tries, no one is listening or cares, or can comprehend it. Annie says this analysis fits well with her experience and is what she has been currently working on in therapy. She is trying to come to terms with the fact that no one, other than a few people in the mental health field and me, will ever understand and accept her for who she is.

"Are you referring to the voices, mostly?" I ask.

"Not just that," she says, "not just the current, day-to-day mental health stuff, but the history of how I came to be who I am. When there's a mental health issue, people just don't want to know about it; they're not interested."

She is trying to figure out what level of this lack of interest she should "settle for" in a close friend or partner. Though I understand the specific meaning of her quandary, it reminds me of the push and pull of most relationships, the degree to which we are willing to reveal ourselves and trust another person to respect the ways we have been wounded, feel most vulnerable, and are different from other people.

* * * * * *

Annie makes living with her voices *look* easy, as if they were nothing more than an interesting icebreaker she might use when asked to reveal something personal about herself, something which makes her instantly unique, but the effort this takes is often so taxing on her inner resources that her muscles and joints "lock up," as she explains it. She must be utterly comfortable with a person to keep the vicious cycle of anxiety and voices from shifting into overdrive. She sometimes wishes she had more friends, but socializing heightens her anxiety. The voices hold side conversations about how worthless or stupid she is—*"Get a load of her! Who does she think she is trying to fit in with these people? Look at how fat and ugly she is!"* Annie says that collectively the voices are like a third person in any relationship, goading, always planting doubt, handicapping her trust. If she is out in public and the voices get too obnoxious, she tries deep breathing to calm herself while attempting not to telegraph her discomfort. The wider web of Annie's acquaintances, though, most likely sees her appealing persona—attractive, funny, stylish, friendly. But the façade feels "fake," she says. I tell her it is necessary and useful. As Berta Britz says, "*Act 'as if'... *"

* * * * * *

At a Montgomery County Hearing Voices Network event, Berta emphasized the importance of *negotiating* with the voices. Like Annie's voices, Berta's have been mostly distressing and abusive, and she spent most of her life afraid of them. When she connected with the Hearing Voices Movement, people like Ron Coleman and Karen Taylor offered her a different path—curiosity. With their support, Berta learned to be curious about the voices instead of afraid, although she admits this is not easy and should not be done alone: "It's really hard to stay open to learning about voices that seem so negative. To do that kind of 'curious dialogue,' I believe we need supporters, in a group and/or individually. When helpers are as scared by the voices as voice hearers are, they teach us to fight and suppress, and that makes recovery harder and slower. It was very rapid for me once I engaged with Karen and Ron and learned from others in the Movement."

Annie attests to the difficulties of remaining open to the voices when they can be so consistently brutish:

Annie: It's not easy to challenge the voices. At the end of the day, I'm the one living with the voices. If they start screaming at me because I've challenged them, I'm the one who has to live with them. They can beat up on you, so mostly, I just try to keep the peace.

But curiosity, according to Berta, leads to an open heart and mind and the opportunity for understanding. By having a more open and vulnerable relationship with her voices, Berta was eventually able to ask them for something she desperately needed—some quiet and intermittent peace—which the voices gave her. She felt transformed through this process and saw herself for the first time as "human." When someone in the audience asked her to elaborate on what she meant by "feeling human," she stated that during the decades she spent subjugated by her voices, she perceived herself as an unnatural entity, a toxin, the begetter of harm and doom. She felt personally and irrationally responsible for the destruction around her, natural disasters, things she could not possibly have had anything to do with. Annie, too, has experienced this surreal kind of guilt ever since her OCD fears in second grade, and she relates to Berta's feeling of not being human.

Annie says she feels "an ocean of difference" between the way she experiences life and the way others do.

"In what way do you not feel human?" I asked her.

"How I feel things, how my mind works, how I love ... it makes it hard for me to believe I'm part of the same human race."

"How do you love differently?"

"With the people I love the most, I worry the most. Don't think for a second that it's just about the voices. Everything is intertwined. I can be thinking, boy, I have a great relationship with Mom, and I feel happy for a minute, and then I'm thinking, but do I? And then I get anxious, and then I'm fearing that you're going to die and this could be the last thing I ever say to you, and then the voices work on that, and then the anxiety spirals and I get depressed, too, and then I feel like I don't want to live my life, I'm going to be here alone, and then I have to pull myself away from everything and isolate, and then I feel manic and can't calm down and I question everything. And, always, I'm consumed by thoughts of death."

* * * * * *

Perhaps because Annie's voices started when she was only twelve years old, she is not as afraid of them as she might be had they started later, when she was more fully formed in her identity and had more to lose in terms of the life she was building. In comparison to many of the voice hearers with whom she comes in contact, she has had more time to reconcile her existence with them. Though she has had so little peace from them, I sometimes feel worse for those young people who suddenly veer off the tracks in college or later, those overwhelmed by their voices just as they are preparing to strike out on their own. The families of these individuals might feel comforted by recollections of more halcyon years, but the shock of the juxtaposition must be heartbreaking to reckon with. Whatever age people start to hear voices, though, we know they came without warning and unbidden. The voices manifested one day and life was never the same.

Chapter 23

"Being identified for hearing voices often means being discredited, prevented from climbing career ladders, and losing the faith of even our friends and family. In many cases, the discrimination against hearing voices causes more pain than the actual experience. Due to these very real social costs, many people who hear voices will not tell family or friends about their experiences and will suffer in silence trying to figure out what is happening to them. If hearing voices was as openly talked about as being left-handed, then all of this suffering would be easily preventable. In reality, voice hearers are pretty cool, and society is missing out on some amazing stories from the community. Also, if we had better tools and support, then those who hear voices could contribute more to their friends, family members, employers, and to society as a whole. The true help of our loved ones, instead of their fear, would go a long way to make the experience okay."

Life with Voices, Dmitriy Gutkovich

I once attended a "Voices Learning Group," an assembly open to voice hearers and anyone else interested in learning about voices. A young woman sat down next to me dressed in elegant corporate attire. She described to the group the difficult time she was having deciding whether to confide to her Human Resources department her "disability" of hearing voices. The strain of having to appear unflappably professional each day was affecting her job performance. I found myself in deep sympathy with her, remembering how I once struggled over a similar decision and how terrifying and unsafe it felt to contemplate exposing myself at work as a mentally struggling individual. This woman's honesty and vulnerability inspired me to share my own experience, and she hugged me when I was done. Others in the room chimed in, and we had a stimulating discussion about privacy and mental health. Whether we consider disclosing the fact that we hear voices or that we may be on the verge of a complete nervous collapse, that choice hinges upon the hope that we will be met on the other end with understanding and compassion.

* * * * * *

Annie has said at Ron Coleman conferences that she is "more than" her voices. She acknowledges the huge impact they have on her life, but she says she cannot afford to pay them too close attention. She can usually tune them out enough to function in her daily life, but occasionally she crumples with anxiety, spirals downward, and sees her life as an endless quagmire of psychological trials. Yet she has come far. She has reestablished broken relationships and learned to curb her rage. She sometimes articulates dreams for herself in a matter-of-fact fashion she has not done since early childhood. We spend much of our time together now, compatible friends rather than dueling adversaries, although every once in a while a tempest blows through and I am reminded of our worst times.

We have attended several "World Hearing Voices Congresses" over the years, each time held in a different country. These are informative, inspiring events filled with speeches, workshops, and small group discussions, all centered around the topic of hearing voices. During the first of these Congresses, I was moved to tears when the moderator, in her opening remarks, performed a roll call of the various countries represented. At first, this exercise seemed like a routine drill to rally the troops, but as countries from Iceland to Japan to Brazil checked in, I was overcome with emotion reflecting on Annie's long and lonely journey culminating in such a rousing moment of kinship from around the world.

On our way home from the Congress, Annie told me her voices were "not thrilled" to attend the event because "*they don't buy into the Movement. They think it's hooey.*" I could not help laughing and asked her why she thought the voices felt that way. She said it was probably because they always wanted to be in control, and in the congenial, accepting atmosphere of the Congress, their dominance was threatened. The voices, she also said, were "*not in favor*" of her "*taking back any power,*" the catchphrase of the hearing voices peer support groups. But viewing Annie's voices through the HVM lens was a game-changer for both of us. The ability to grasp hearing voices as part of the diversity of the human experience and not as the symptom of a defective brain was a momentous step in both our lives. I laud the potential of effective psychiatric medication to eradicate voices, but if the best it can do for most voice hearers is slightly dampen their distressing voices at the high cost of disabling side effects, I like to think the HVM's approach might help mitigate their suffering and offer a more appealing model of recovery.

In Annie's case, it may be that the overlay of trauma upon her genetic temperament was a plausible blueprint for the development of voices. She has never fully recovered from her traumas, and medication has never demonstrated any "lock-and-key" improvement in her symptoms. Although she stayed in therapy with Jean for ten years, she sometimes still feels like "one big open wound." But our psychological responses to trauma are unpredictable, so much depending upon the trauma itself and the person who experiences it. Some individuals, endowed with a sunny disposition, raised in a stable, nurturing environment, blessed with a strong network of support, might be capable of con-fronting trauma head-on and never be driven to the extreme defense of voices; other more highly sensitive people, or those scarred from chaotic upbringings or grinding poverty, might struggle more to cope. An individual's age at the time of trauma, as well as the amount of time "allowed" to process it, are also major factors in how our defenses roll out, when survival stratagems like voices might be called into action.

Hearing voices *is* surprisingly more common than we think, though, and it behooves us as a society to learn as much as we can from those who hear them, not only for the betterment of our mental health services but so that we can *all* treat each other as humanely as possible. Here, Annie describes a little more about her experience, which gives some insight into how the voices affect her cognitive processes and her life:

Annie: It would be nice if there wasn't such a stigma and discrimination about voices, but there is. It's not universal enough that people understand. It's uncomfortable to talk about them. People just think of schizophrenia, that you're crazy, and I would rather not have people look at me that way. The traumatic things that happened to me took a deep psychological toll, and people just don't have an understanding of how that affects a person.

There's a piece of the voices that's protective of me, in a twisted way. They want to be the only ones to treat me badly, but if anyone else does that, they encourage me not to take it. 'Are you going to take that from them?' they'll say. They want to be the only ones allowed to speak to me in that mean way. They like to have the control.

Overall, it's just a melting pot of everything; it's my nature, it's the experiences, it's my surroundings. I think I went through the worst of my stuff early on, and I can tune out the voices better than most now. Life goes on with or without the voices. I know I have to live my life and make a decent income. I do think I'm mature for my age, but I resent the fact that the mental health stuff stunted my growth. I couldn't develop interests or friend-ships at the time everyone else was. I didn't know who I was outside of the whole mental health world. Social interactions never came naturally to me. I never felt like I fit in. Even before Sister Maria, I had the guilt and anxiety; the religious stuff just validated those feelings, just magnified everything. I felt like I was a bad person. But I could also be a happy kid and I always wanted to help people.

The voices are a part of me now. I might even miss them if they were gone. They're company, and even though they're mean to me a lot of the time, I know in a way they're looking out for me.

Chapter 24

> "I am afraid to tell you who I am, because if I tell you
> who I am, you may not like who I am, and it's all
> that I have."

Why Am I Afraid to Tell You Who I Am? John Powell, S.J.

In the late fall and winter of 2021-22, when Annie was twenty-five years old, and our country was emerging from the worst of the Covid-19 pandemic, she reached a dangerously low point in her mental health struggles. Though she was still able to land entry-level jobs quickly, she was finding it nearly impossible to hold one down. She left one job after another, backing herself into an ever-narrower corner with fewer and fewer options. She was nearing completion of her associate's degree when she was stymied by her old nemesis, mathematics. It was a gargantuan feat for her to get through even the most remedial math class, and she was ready to throw in the towel. Her personal life, too, was in shambles. The few friendships she had fizzled out, she had made a painful final break with her on-again-off-again boyfriend, and she had become more and more reliant on alcohol to cope with the "brutality in her mind," as she put it. The persistent murmur of suicidal ideation thrumming in her mind was now a thundering chorus tempting her to end it all. She saw no reason to keep living, she said, because she could not envision either her life's circumstances or her mental condition ever improving. She spoke only of hopelessness and said it was "futile to keep trying."

She often exclaimed over the years, *"Over my dead body will I ever return to inpatient treatment!"* but early on a cold January morning, having had way too much to drink the night before, she burst into my room and cried, *"I need to go somewhere, and if I don't go now, I don't know what I'll do. I need to go now! Take me to the hospital. I can't take this anymore!"*

Annie frequently smoked marijuana at night to get to sleep. She knew I disapproved, but whenever I brought it up, she acknowledged why it might upset me but refused to apologize for using the only substance that had ever given her a sliver of relief from the voices and her anxiety. Her argument gave me pause, and I tried not to debate the issue with her. I thought she had given it up for a while, though, when I then realized her drinking had gotten out of control. I knew she kept bottles of alcohol stashed in her drawer, and I often detected a faint whiff on her breath, but it was not obvious, and if I dared to comment on it, she nearly blew my head off. But there came an evening when she finally validated my concerns. I think it was one of the hardest things she ever did.

My compassion toward substance abuse did not come as easily to me as it did for mental health issues, but I tried to listen to her pain and understand her compulsion without judging the behavior. She was ashamed of her drinking and said she was not able to stop once she started, the way other people were. She told me she was having repeated dreams warning her that alcohol would be her downfall and knew that it was time to get a handle on it. She would keep an eye on it, she assured me, and I think she did try, as much as she could, but she was so bowed down with misery during this time that she grew more reckless by the day. I seldom saw her when she was flat-out drunk, but one afternoon I came home from work to find her slurring so badly she could hardly keep her head up. A couple of weeks after that, she was desperate to be hospitalized.

When we arrived at the Emergency Room, the crisis intervention worker was eager to get Annie admitted to a "dual-diagnosis" treatment facility. While she called around for a "bed" in our area, Annie waited in the holding area for much of the day before eventually signing herself out. Those hours gave her time to reflect on how traumatizing hospitalizations had always been for her, and she came back around to the vow she once made to stay out of mental health facilities for her "own mental health."

It was understandable and expected that the crisis worker urged her to first "get clean," but Annie felt that the "dual-diagnosis" label gave a false impression of the real issues. Though the rate of co-occurring mental health and substance use disorder is extremely high—45 percent of individuals with addiction problems have a co-occurring mental health disorder, according to the National Survey on Drug Use and Health (NSDUH)—Annie felt that her emotional issues were driving her desperation to drink and that if she could get a better grip on her overall mental health, the diminution of despair would naturally slake the desire to escape through substances. And thus began our very frustrating and disheartening search for adult mental health services.

* * * * * *

Annie, Mike, and I reached out to every contact we had for recommendations on psychiatrists and psychologists and researched any treatment center in our area. Since her longtime therapist had retired, Annie was "trying on" new ones; however, Jean knew her so well, and they had done so much good work together, including work with the voices, it was hard for her to find anyone as skilled or as open-minded about the voices. Even more difficult was finding a psychiatrist. Anyone who seemed remotely promising was not taking on new patients, would not accept our insurance, or both. Suddenly, the Medicaid insurance that had been so valuable in the past was now a disadvantage to Annie. As soon as a potential service provider heard she had Medicaid, she was rejected. Long waiting lists for psychologists and psychiatrists and appointments scheduled weeks and months in the future were the norm. Out-of-pocket costs were prohibitive, but Annie kept a few of these appointments hoping she might stumble on a gem and figure out the rest later.

There was a mental health "day program" at a nearby behavioral health facility, which Annie tried, but she did not last through the first morning because it felt to her like "the same old stuff" she hated. There were a few part-time dual-diagnosis programs in our area, but because she had not been through an inpatient stay first, she was not accepted. On the other hand, the inpatient dual-diagnosis facilities we investigated hounded Annie by phone, eager to take my primary insurance; however, their daily co-pays were exorbitant, their reviews and outcomes data were poor, and Annie was not even willing to enter one. We considered ECT, transcranial magnetic stimulation, ketamine infusion therapy, and any other treatment modalities we learned about, but they felt like stopgap solutions outside the context of the more comprehensive treatment programs we could not afford.

With the Covid-related rise in telehealth psychiatric care, we contacted out-of-state professionals recommended to us. One psychiatrist we were familiar with through the Hearing

Voices Movement responded with a compassionate email but was unable to treat Annie remotely because of the state-by-state licensing laws. It was the same situation with the other out-of-state psychiatrists we reached out to.

While most of the professionals Annie met with during this period were well-meaning, some had a bedside manner she could not warm to. When she admitted to one psychiatrist that she had never taken a medication that actually helped her, the woman responded, *"Really? Well, why are you even here, then?"* Hardly an assertion of hope and encouragement. On another occasion, a psychologist Annie waited weeks to see referred to herself as a "straight shooter," and said she knew exactly what Annie needed. Then she quickly proceeded to cast doubt on a traumatic event Annie shared, without tact or the slightest buildup of trust or empathy. When Annie got home from that appointment, she was crying and furious at how presumptuous the therapist had been. She said she "shut down" within ten minutes of the conversation and then humored the therapist until it was over. After that experience, we decided that Annie might just have to do the hard work herself, without waiting for the "right" person to facilitate her recovery.

This brings us to the present date, at which point Annie can tell her own story:

> ***ANNIE:*** *I have navigated many trying years, but none as difficult as these most recent ones, in my mid-twenties.*
>
> *While I do not hide my mental illness, there is much of my experience that I fiercely safeguard. I shield this part of myself largely due to profound shame but also for fear of rejection. If I do not talk about it, I cannot be misunderstood or judged. But inherent in this isolation is a disconnection from anyone really knowing me, a feeling that I would not wish upon anyone. I am still on the front lines fighting this battle, but I will do my best to share what I can as articulately as possible.*

In November 2021, after a tumultuous five-year relationship finally came to a definitive end, I was shattered. It had been years of on-and-off struggle, a rollercoaster ride that was slowly killing me. While I was not mentally well prior to the breakup, by the conclusion of that relationship, whatever fragile equilibrium I had achieved was annihilated. It is important for me to note that my downward trajectory was not the direct result of our separation; that would be an oversimplification. The breakup was the predecessor, the final nail in the coffin to a breakdown that had been boiling below the surface for years. Throughout our relationship, I had created a barrier between myself and the excruciating challenges I lived with. They were not necessary to face while I had the distraction of this relationship. With this barrier now removed, the floodgates opened, and there was nothing I could do to stop it.

I began to spiral.

Most days, I was mournful and struggled to move from the couch, wondering, "what's the point, anyway?" Other days, I oozed bitter rage, and was a true nightmare for my mother to be around. I cried often and barely slept. Physically, it felt like my body was shutting down. The typical anxiety, depression, panic, voices, and obsessive compulsions that I juggled on a daily basis had become insufferable. The entire situation was embarrassing, even. I had survived the loss of my childhood at seven years old, overcome numerous traumas, navigated deplorable conditions during residential and inpatient hospitalizations, and been separated from those I loved, but now a man was going to be what buried me?! Nonetheless, no matter how hard I tried, I could not shake it. I came to learn that broken hearts and mental illness are a dangerous combination.

At the start of my 20s, I realized that alcohol was the only tool I had to effectively loosen the chokehold of my anxiety. When I drank, I was better. I could be in social settings, speak more freely, and most importantly, relax. My partner and I's favorite activity had been to indulge in *this habit, and over our five years together, I found myself drinking more frequently and in larger amounts than ever before. Partly, the foggy state masked underlying issues in our relationship. But also, I believed that I needed to be drunk to be "normal." In the aftermath of our breakup, my depression was all-consuming. I craved the reprieve from suffering that I received through alcohol, desperate for mental refuge. I began to drink with a vengeance. Although unhealthy, alcohol has provided me comfort when no other person, medication, or treatment could. Unfortunately, this relief comes at a steep price.*

When my mother gently confided in me one night that she was concerned about my drinking, I was forced to confront my vice. This was not the first time that she had approached me about the topic. I validated her concern; there was no denying that this was harmful behavior. But it felt important for her to understand why I drank. Living with such constant inner torment, no friends or human connection outside my home, was too much. At this point, alcohol was the only thing that was keeping me from ending my life. In my gut, I knew that alcohol was not the root problem but a symptom.

If I could ever finally, finally, find a "legal" medication that was effective in taking the edge off, alcohol would not be such a necessary crutch. I knew the drinking was an issue; I just could not do anything about it right now. Miraculously, my mother understood. She shared her heartache that things were so difficult right now. She would take it all away if she could, she said. However, one last time my mother emphasized her concern that I should not travel too deeply down this path. She had witnessed addiction first-hand, how it can ravage a person and a whole family. My mother did not want this pain for me. And now I understood. Filled with gratitude for her trust in me, I vowed to keep an eye on it.

Six months prior, I had decided to conclude work with my therapist of over ten years. She was a compassionate woman who had been the only silver lining to come from my time in a group home, and we continued therapy together for many years after. Now twenty-five, I felt that our time together had run its natural course. While confident in this decision, the newfound absence of therapy left a gaping hole in my sparse support system. I could not imagine starting this relationship all over with someone new. Additionally, I was especially overwhelmed by the need to find a therapist who would respect my unique circumstances. However daunting, at this crisis point, it felt critical to try.

Another essential piece of the puzzle was to find a psychiatrist. Someone who accepted that I did not desire to be a zombie but needed strong enough medication to control my constant panic. Someone who understood that, yes, while I heard voices, this was not the most distressing symptom that I was seeking treatment for. Someone who acknowledged that the mental health system had fundamentally traumatized me for too long and that at this stage of my life, I wanted to make the decisions about what was best for me. Each day I spent hours placing phone calls to various therapists and psychiatry organizations. Rarely did I reach a live person, forced instead to leave detailed messages regarding the urgency of my situation and pleading for a callback. On the off chance that I did receive that returned call, it was simply to say, "Unfortunately, we don't take your insurance. Good luck."

Growing increasingly desperate, we concluded it was necessary to apply for state Medicaid insurance, confident that this supplemental coverage would open more doors. Once approved, Medicaid actually made it more difficult to obtain treatment. Most agencies refused to accept me as a client with Medicaid as my secondary insurance. The ones that did still required astronomical co-pays that we could not possibly afford. Although it was insurance that posed the biggest hurdle, there were several other factors that complicated accessing services.

Many agencies require clients to utilize both a psychiatrist and therapist within their organization. While I could respect the desired autonomy, I was uncomfortable with this and felt it took away my agency. Other times, I was flippantly questioned by potential providers, "well, if nothing works, why are you even here?" Coldly, I would counter, "Because I have to believe there is a better way to live than this." Finally, if somewhere was open to treating me and appeared relatively financially feasible, their first availability was not until months out. I hung up the phone and started wailing like a wounded animal. I would be long dead by then.

Adamant about not wanting to be admitted as an inpatient due to prior detrimental experiences, partial hospitalization felt like the next appropriate level of care. We rushed arrangements with a local hospital provider, and the following Monday morning, I nervously arrived at the center at 8 AM. Immediately upon entering its doors, I was overwhelmed by the stagnant, sterile air and endless beige décor. Where were the windows? The color? The warmth? My throat began to close. I knew I had made a grave mistake.

I was quickly ushered into a stuffy side office. A staff member began pelting me with questions. "Why are you here? What are your symptoms? Are you suicidal? Do you hear voices? Do you drink? What is your trauma history?" Whiplash, I shut down. I had not been in the building for more than ten minutes before I was ordered to disclose the most vulnerable parts of myself to this stranger, to whom I represented only data. Every word out of her mouth put me off more than the last. I responded curtly, with answers bathed in bitterness. Disassociating, I floated above my body and helplessly watched the scene unfold from below me.

Once the inquisition had ceased, it was time to join the others. The next room I entered contained a handful of individuals, ranging from young children to elderly adults, all positioned in a circle. Apparently, we had been instructed to share our feelings. Most members clamored to be the loudest voice in the room, sharing arbitrary ramblings of what had been eaten for breakfast or about a new video game they were playing. The others' blatant eyeballing of me was palpable as they waited for me to reveal my skeletons and prove that I was messed up enough to belong there. I sat back and said nothing. After a lengthy monologue from a woman who told us, "We're all just made of stardust, man," and an elderly patient who talked about her cat for upward of twenty minutes, I was done. The partial program was over for me before it ever began.

When lunch break hit, I booked it out of the building, sucking in every bit of fresh air from the outside world that I could. I heard myself repeating the words "you're so stupid" over and over; this program never held a chance for me as a good fit. Racing down the highway toward home, I finally began to relax. Freedom.

So neither inpatient treatment nor partial hospitalization was the answer. My options were running out.

After my most recent failure, I was convinced I needed to shift gears. Maybe I had been approaching this all wrong, I thought. What I craved was stability, consistency, and a sense of purpose. I tried to reflect upon points in my life when I had experienced such emotions. As a high school student with a steady part-time job, I had felt so proud. To earn my own money and be part of a community had been exhilarating. But most importantly, I had had a reason to get out of bed—my work was counting on me. Although in recent years, any attempts at employment had been wildly unsuccessful, I was determined to try again.

The merry-go-round began. For every failed attempt at work, there was a unique reason that the position proved unsuccessful. Hostess, too stressful. Cashier, too much math. Patient transport for a hospital, too overwhelming. Receptionist, too draining. Retail associate, too slow. Counter sales, too fast. It did not matter what the job was, my mental illness interfered. I wanted to work; I did. I liked to work. Unfortunately, though, when triggered, my anxiety flipped into high gear, and it was fight or flight. When it came to employment, I chose flight. This tendency created an exhaustive cycle of burned bridges and took an immense emotional toll on my family and me. Finally, I reached a miserable conclusion. As much as I wanted to be "normal" and have a job, it was not in the cards right now. I could not live like other people and needed to accept it. This realization prompted the deeply difficult decision to file an application for Social Security Disability Benefits. I waved the white flag.

I was defeated. I was a failure. Unlovable. Broken and not meant for this world. Drinking heavily, I descended into blackness to escape the pain. There are many nights that I do not remember. In many situations, it's a miracle I survived safely, men that I gave myself to because they merely looked my way. While my memory failed me, the staggering pit of shame the next mornings was paralyzing. I hated myself. As desperately as I drank to forget my demons, this cycle only piled on more pain and regret. "You're so stupid," the voices told me, "You worthless idiot!" The shadows under my eyes were getting darker by the day.

Throughout my crisis, I continued to talk to my mother. I told her that I did not know how much longer I could do this; every breath hurt to be alive. She cried with me and stroked my hair like when I was a child, quietly reminding me that I could not leave her here on earth alone. That we needed each other. There was not much in this life that I was certain of, but one thing that had always anchored me was that I could not leave my mother to grieve a deceased child. Otherwise, I would have checked out a long time ago. But no, she had endured far too much in her years. I could not add that to the list. However, it terrified me how this principal rule of mine was fading. Suddenly, I was drafting goodbye letters to my family and was transfixed by the pill bottles that surrounded me. How easily I could end my suffering. "It will be hard for my mother," I thought, "but she will understand why I had to do this." I could feel my fight slipping away.

After an especially bad bender in the city, I crawled home and told my mother that I needed help. While treatment for alcoholism was not ultimately the support I felt I most needed; it was a piece of the puzzle. We went to the emergency room. Shaking and delirious, I uncomfortably attempted to articulate my struggles with alcohol for the first time to the endless number of hospital personnel who filtered in and out of the room. Everyone had an opinion to offer. They stated that rehab was what I "need" and some shared their own experiences of addiction with me, how it was rehab that had changed their trajectory. That's nice, I thought, but how do you know what I need? What is best for me, personally?

The flashbacks flooded in. I squeezed my eyes shut tight to try and make it stop. Had these hospital workers spent years caught in a revolving door of psychiatric hospitals, under lock and key and force-fed medication? Witnessed the horrors of out-of-home placement that I had? The corruption and absence of free will? I desperately wished the hospital staff would stop referencing this path of treatment like it was easy because it was not easy. I had sworn to myself that I would never be in this position again. However, I had no other options. Maybe this time would be different...

My skin felt itchy. As nine hours went by, I began to panic. Any inclination to take a leap of faith had long passed, and I knew in my gut that rehab was not a fit for me. The only support that I had in my entire life was in the safety of my home with my mother. To remove that foundation would very well put me over the edge. The hospital staff forcefully asserted that I was making the wrong decision to not go to treatment and that I would not succeed on my own. I did not expect them to understand. I promised to seek the help that I knew I needed in a manner that would be less harmful to my mental health. Still, they continued to work on me, but I would not be swayed. I am the only one in my body, and I know what is best for me. This was not it.

When I arrived home from the emergency room, I was lost. Immediately, I began to pursue the intensive outpatient programs that the hospital had suggested for my drinking. Unfortunately, each one informed me that I must have completed thirty days of rehab to be admitted. Well, there goes that. I tried attending Alcoholics Anonymous meetings where no one showed up. When I did find an active meeting, I was overwhelmed by the aggressive prompting from others to get my hand up and share. I was not ready. Between the amount of people, social pressure, and expectation to speak, the meetings were too much for me to handle. I left feeling even lonelier than when I arrived. After enough times, I stopped trying.

I went back to drinking. This time, I felt ready to let it kill me. I had exhaustively tried to play by the rules and seek proper help for my depression and anxiety, but all roads led to nowhere. The emergency room worker had advised, "You know, when mental illness is a factor, it all comes down to the right medication! You should have a psychiatrist!" I wanted to spit, leap across the bed and yank her hair out. As if it was possibly that easy, as if I had not been trying! Frantically, my mother and I considered more extreme options, such as electroconvulsive therapy, transcranial magnetic stimulation, and ketamine infusions. I even cried that I would get a lobotomy if I could. Anything to make the pain, the darkness, subside. I needed relief, but nothing worked. But drinking did, so I chose to drink.

After my experiences trying to get the right help, not only in the last few months but over the course of my life, I decided I was finished with the mental health system. We did not see eye to eye, the system and me. I had never fit into their neat little box of what a client should be. While I had been receptive to help over the years, I had also refused to conform to treatment plans that I did not agree with or diminish the value of my own lived experience. The ways my illness manifested were not convenient to how the system operated. Because of this, I earned the titles "difficult" and "treatment resistant." But I would not let these labels haunt me any longer. I was going to claw my way out of this hole. I would have to do it myself.

I began an independent study. Extensively, I researched alternative practices such as reiki, massage therapy, spiritual retreats, acupuncture, and trauma-based yoga. I considered what physical outlets could be beneficial: boxing to release pent-up anger and dance classes to let loose. I even enrolled in a figure skating program, which was one of my favorite hobbies as a child. This was also when I had my transformational experience with a psychic. I sought to reconnect with my younger self. Because that girl was so full of life and dreams, maybe she was still in there somewhere, deep down. Maybe, if I protected her and promised that from now on, we were in this together, she could be brave enough to step forward again.

I knew that an essential missing ingredient from my recipe for healing was writing. I used to write to survive. Stacks of marble composition notebooks still line my closet containing narratives of bleak adolescent years and my time spent in the hospital. Writing was my lifeline and my only constant. Writing was my friend, and when I put pen to paper, I was home. I wanted to find that home again more than anything, but I was stuck.

For so many years, I had driven the same suburban streets. I passed the same graveyard of failed jobs, schools that were the backdrop for misery, and bars that I had anxiously blacked out in. Each day as I pass these sites, I fill up with the same familiar shame, and it knocks the wind out of my chest. When my peers left for college, moved away, or set out to study abroad, I stayed put. I have always stayed here. I was okay with that. The milestones that others achieved were not my path. But as the list of painful landmarks to avoid has become longer and longer, my world has become smaller and smaller. So small that I now felt trapped. Like I am condemned to these confines as punishment for my many sins. I desperately needed a reminder that there was life outside of what I knew.

"Where is the best place to travel alone for the first time? Which destinations have the cheapest airfare? What is a pretty location to go in early spring? How to get around in a city with limited transportation?" Furiously, I typed such questions into Google's search bar and pondered the results. Europe was a recurring theme for solo expeditions, but I was not comfortable navigating abroad independently. New Orleans? Very tempting, but with the nightlife there, I would never make it out alive. Chicago? Not right now, too cold. I would like my getaway to be scenic, pleasant in temperature, not too far from water, manageable... Google pinged Charleston. I sat back. Charleston?

Charleston, yes, I liked the sound of this. I was taking a vacation to Charleston; I would be back soon. The rows of pastel-painted historic homes that were displayed on the computer screen were mesmerizing, mansions settled on cobblestone walkways and protected by fluffy palm trees. Delicious food, stunning beaches, and even the possibility of meeting a southern gentleman made me giddy. I found the most affordable flight I could, secured reasonable accommodations, took a deep breath, and pressed "Book." Charleston, here I come!

The plan was to utilize this upcoming trip as a creative retreat—another form of alternative healing. I believed that the excitement of a new city could kick start my "breakthrough" in exactly the way I had been looking for. I planned to immerse myself in a sea of reading material I had collected, tackle workbooks on how to move past complex trauma, and make substantial progress on my writing each day. Without the distracting pain of my hometown, I believed that the potential for this excursion was limitless. This would be my first real step toward independence, and nothing could stop me.

My parents knew that I was romanticizing the trip; we had traveled such a path many times before. The shiny discovery that finally, here it was, the answer! Nonetheless, they supported my plan. Both emphasized that I was taking on a lot, and if it became too much, if I was uncomfortable or distressed, there was no shame in ending my trip early. If I needed him, my father would be on the next flight out, he said. My heart swelled with love for these two people, these two incredible parents who still championed their unstable daughter even amid all her ill-fated endeavors. How they still held hope that maybe this time would be different.

Long story short, it was not different. The trip was a disaster. I barely made it out of the airport, let alone one night in Charleston, before I decided to come home. However, from this failed excursion to enlightenment, I gained more insight than I ever could have anticipated. I discovered that it does not matter where you go; you will always take yourself with you. That the hard work of healing can be completed right in your own backyard if you are ready to take the steps. And to achieve your ambitions, it takes time— long, messy time.

I arrived at the Charleston airport to come home to Philadelphia hours early. I could not help but feel dejected that I was about to leave South Carolina without ever having seen the outside of my dingy hotel walls. Once I checked my luggage, a strange wave of bravery took over. I decided to call a Lyft and ride into downtown Charleston. Once there, I dined at one of the restaurants I had carefully planned on my itinerary and enjoyed my first authentic southern meal. Afterward, I took a stroll through Charleston's picturesque main street and even stopped for an ice cream cone—butter pecan. I smiled. Maybe I was not so helpless after all. Now it was time to go home.

So while my trip was a failure, it was also the farthest thing from that.

I wish that I could conclude my saga with more optimism. However, each day, I take tiny steps to better myself. I continue to try to resist the darkness that wants to pull me in, some days with more success than others. And just when

I think I might finally be making progress, I break down and collapse into a million little pieces. It is only with sheer willpower and the help of my family, my mother, that I am eventually able to get back up again. I place one trembling foot in front of the other and wobble out into the world once more, eyes blinking at the sun like a newborn fawn, as if for the first time. Fall, get up. Fall, get up.

Many weeks later, there are several updates to my mental health journey I can now offer:

I am slowly but surely building a support network, however unconventional it may be. For example, there is my primary care physician, a gentle man who stepped up and treated me with more dignity and trust than I have ever encountered. My dentist, whom I have known since childhood and continues to extend acts of kindness however she can. But most importantly, I found a nurse practitioner to help treat some of my debilitating symptoms. I finally found her! A shot-in-the-dark appointment. A bohemian woman who blew me away from the first visit. Present, empathetic, trustful, and generous with her support. We are learning together how best to treat me. Maybe, just maybe, I have a chance.

Nothing good will come from my continuing to drink. I have accepted that remaining sober is a daily battle. I attempt to utilize Alcoholics Anonymous meetings for support, but my social anxiety still critically interferes. I hope eventually this will change. While I still do not know what the best help for my addiction looks like, I do know that I do not want to be this version of myself any longer, that girl who I cannot bear to face in the mirror. One day at a time.

Developing spirituality will be a crucial part of my healing. After what I experienced in second grade, I abandoned my belief in the afterlife. If there was a higher power, why did it cause me so much pain? The unknown was crippling, and the end was just that—the end. Through the process of honing my connection to the other world, I am slowly learning to trust again. To reclaim my childlike conviction that my departed loved ones and I will be reunited someday and that they are watching over me, guiding me every day. I will try not to be afraid of what comes next.

I continue to advocate for mental health system reform at every opportunity. However, I refuse to be part of a system that oppressed me and will not play a role in someone else's institutional trauma.

I feel a tremendous pressure to reach the potential that others have generously identified in me over the years, to reach the potential that I see in myself. While it is unclear if I will ever fulfill my lofty ambitions, I know that I owe it to myself, to the village of people who have helped me along the way, and to the rest of the world to try.

I am hardened, but I am soft.

I am bad, but I am good.

I am lost, but I am found.

I am lonely, but with my mother, I am never alone.

MOTHER

Afterward

Occasionally, I mourn the divided nature of my family, yet it is the course our lives took. Mike does not live with us, but he is our strongest ally, the first one to help in any crisis, large or small. He struggled with his own "dark night of the soul" and is now a sincere born-again Christian, which has given him great sustenance and fellowship. Annie loves him and has been gracious and respectful of his experiences, but she also admits that at times his religious conversion is "hard to take" considering the fundamentalist indoctrination he once fought so hard against. Though she sharply demarcates the boundaries of their relationship, refraining from any serious talk of mental health issues with him, their father-daughter attachment is otherwise strong and provides the comfort and support any child needs.

In recent years, I was caught up short to learn I had committed other parental infractions. After years of attention focused on Annie, my son Joe, in his mid-twenties, commenced his own pilgrimage through therapy and got in touch with his own packet of grievances. Worst of them was that I had not spent enough time getting to know him, had not poked behind his shield of humor. I was surprised; I had mistakenly, or conveniently, thought our relationship was a good one and was even somewhat proud of it. I knew it was not as emotionally deep as the one I had with Annie, but I assumed he preferred it that way, without heavy discussions and inept attempts to bond with him. But the truth was I found it difficult to crack Joe's shell; he was introverted, like me, and I instinctively dropped back, as I always had, afraid of rejection. *"But why would I reject you?"* he wondered. I was defensive and told him he usually did not respond to my overtures of conversation. The examples I gave to prove how much I loved him came to nothing in his mind. He also said he had no idea who I was as a person. *"I don't know anything about you!"* he stated. In the end, I had to admit that to some degree, I did the familiar, damaging thing, left him alone, relieved for this less demanding child amid the more trying circumstances at home.

When Joe was young and my mother was alive, I asked her if she thought he would remember how fiercely I had loved him, if the countless little ways we treasure our children, things we know they will never recall, really make a difference in the long run, and she exclaimed, "Of course, they do!" But those early years, when I knew I had given him my best, were only part of the story. I had to face the fact that even my "good enough" parenting had not been good enough *for him.* I should have stepped out of myself and pushed harder to build a deeper connection with him, especially during his sullen middle-school years, especially when he had difficulties with Mike, especially during high school when he pushed me away from him and his friends, especially when the marriage broke up and Annie was the one who required me to grow up.

Again, the recognition that I had failed as a mother, with both my children, nearly undid me. One day I found an old application Joe once submitted for an out-of-state teaching job. "I have an intolerable situation at home," he wrote. His unhappiness stunned me, and I clutched my stomach in pain. At one point, I wanted to hurt myself, punish myself, clawing at the skin around my neck until it almost bled. I needed to externalize my pain and finally understood the allure of self-harming behavior. I needed help and re-entered therapy. There were amends to be made on my part and tough discussions to be worked through. He was brave and vulnerable; I resolved not to be defeated by the past but to do better in the future.

Yet how daunting this parenting business is! By the time we suspect we may not be constitutionally fit for the job, we have young lives dependent upon the mettle of our character. The weight of the responsibility can be onerous. Had I known then the deficiencies I know now, I might not have risked it. But I could never regret, and I am profoundly thankful for, the love and optimism that brought these two remarkable, cherished people into my life.

* * * * * *

A woman I once encountered, whose teenage son struggled with hearing voices and other psychological challenges, told me she was certain his condition was the product of a genetic predisposition on her husband's side of the family. She could not bear to see her son in such mental pain and admitted she would not have married into the family had she realized the enormity of the DNA gamble. There were no traces of mental illness on her side of the family, she insisted. She considered the environmental influence an outlier and was convinced not only that destiny was encoded in the genes, but that her son's voices disqualified him from leading any kind of fulfilling life.

I appreciated her honesty, and although I cringed at her grim, deterministic outlook, I could not help but feel slightly blameworthy myself. However, to muse upon a human condition impervious to extreme psychic pain is to imagine a eugenic ideal of humanity devoid of emotional depth, the exquisite sensitivity that gives rise to much of the world's beauty, art, and kindness. I am a realist; I know that Annie's voices affect the quality of her life, but I hope not the depth of contentment she finds one day.

Lastly, please forgive my divulging such a personal account. I have ventured this far out of the mental health shadows because the older I get, the more apparent it seems that our suffering unites us and that our stories are how we soften the pain. We are all entitled to privacy, though, and I have tried to reveal only details in service to the larger framework of mental health.

I could not have survived my crisis, my showdown with the apparition, without psychotherapy, without human acceptance and understanding, without love. And that dash of chemical fortification that medication can provide mollifies me and gives me a tincture of confidence that my body can withstand stress. If you, too, should find yourself in deep emotional turmoil and find a therapist and/or psychiatrist whom you respect and are willing to entrust with your well-being, consider yourself lucky. Allow yourself to be cared for and enjoy the luxury of having someone think deeply about the matters that trouble you. This entails acknowledging your susceptibility to psychological pain, as well as your potential for healing. If a voice hearer should feel less alone, more understood by what has been read here, or if someone with anxiety, depression, obsessive-compulsive disorder, social anxiety disorder, borderline personality disorder, bipolar disorder, schizophrenia, schizoaffective disorder, or any of the other DSM labels recognizes the many commonalities in our very human struggles, our step out of obscurity will have been worth it.

Annie continues to seek the peace that eludes her. She has been humbled and knows she needs help, but she also knows there are no perfect answers or treatments. She has a new awareness that *she* is the prime mover in all her endeavors and is responsible for blazing her own trail to recovery.

To that end, she is working steadily at a part-time job, plugging away at her math courses, and has her sights set on a bachelor's degree in psychology. She has not found a therapist, but she is under the care of an exceptional nurse practitioner. On most days, she writes in her journal for her own enrichment, and she is working on a novel about a character with mental health challenges. She wrestles with the exercises in her DBT (dialectical behavioral therapy) workbook, where she records lengthy, engaging responses. She is not drinking, and occasionally she attends an AA meeting, where she has great trouble with the God talk and the group dynamics. However, she appreciates that small amount of human contact and support, and she tries to stay focused on the program's "steps." She has a shrewd business sense and is fleshing out a plan for a unique establishment she wants to open one day. She benefits physically and mentally from regular workouts at a gym, and she spends time each day training her beautiful golden retriever puppy, who may soon serve as her emotional support dog. In addition, for the past three years, she has been the creative force behind our nonprofit organization called Tend to Hope, whose mission is to inspire hope in individuals in mental health crisis facilities.

None of this is easy. Annie progresses in fits and starts, and all with crippling anxiety, yet I believe that so much constructive effort will stand her in good stead. Some of the better mental health services out there have given her ports in the storm, without which she, or we, might have capsized at sea. We may never cut loose from their moorings, but sometimes on a clear day, the ocean glitters peacefully, and we envision a stretch of smooth sailing.

I would like to leave my daughter with this thought:

"Yes, it is important to make sense of one's personal experiences, to face all of the distressing aspects of one's history, to name the abuses and traumas and neglect, and to own the shame, anger, addictive cravings, and low self-esteem that one's identity has coalesced around as a result. But it is also important to know that one does not have to be defined by these things. To hold them all lightly, the way a mother holds a baby, is to let an underlying, fundamental, and interpersonally entangled benevolence shine through."

Dr. Mark Epstein, The Zen of Therapy

A Final Note from Annie

I do not subscribe to the term "recovery." I am not "in recovery," nor do I believe I ever will be. Over the years, I have been told that a mindset like this could hinder me from making progress. I argue that this mentality has been necessary for me to adapt so I can protect myself from further disappointment. I do not know if I will ever discover the right cocktail of medication or achieve a therapeutic breakthrough that allows me to finally move forward. It is terrifying to imagine I could be perpetually consumed by unmanageable emotions.

I do not experience life the way most people do. Even the most joyful moment, a birthday, a celebration, is painfully tainted with the bitter reminder that nothing lasts forever. I teeter on the edge and try to keep from hyperventilating when I remember that one day I will have to live in a world without my mother. I cannot breathe. There is no compartmentalizing such absolutes; I exist in the past or future, never in the present.

Rather than recover, I seek to heal. To me, healing is not as daunting; there is less of an emphasis on the absence of symptoms. I simply aspire to live authentically and finally strike a balance between who I am behind closed doors and the Annie that the rest of the world encounters. I hope that all my parts of self may find forgiveness for themselves in the same way they are able to extend compassion to others. I want to allow myself to live a full life.

While I honor the progress I have made throughout my journey, this juncture of my life holds different challenges. "You are too old to be struggling like this," my mind taunts. "You should have figured it out by now." I become disheartened and frustrated by the lack of success I have seen in my life. But I try to remind myself that between a predisposition to mental illness and early childhood trauma, I did not really have a fair shot. I do the best that I can.

I long to live a life that I can be proud of, but each day is like a tidal wave crashing down on me, and I struggle to breathe. Head barely above water, I gasp, thrashing about for a life preserver I cannot find. I am sure I am going to drown. But now I find I am learning to paddle. Slowly, cautiously, I tread forward. And one day, maybe I will even be able to swim. Move with ease through the swells, appreciate the warm kiss of the sun on my body, and allow the cool water to cleanse my weary soul—a gentle reminder that tomorrow is another chance.

Together

Transition
Ambition
Imposition
alas, total abolition.
Oh, sixth grade! Oh, sixth grade!
A chance to start new
but some things don't fade
like what you've been through.
The ghosts keep knocking
they won't go away
but now there's a new voice
and it's here to stay.
"You're bad
you're evil
you're going to hell.
Try all you want
we won't be bidding farewell."
So, I cut, and I drank, and I sipped, and I smoked
but no quiet will come
the voices shan't be revoked.
"Ha, ha! Look, see! We told you, it's us in charge now
there's no sense in trying
you're ours forever
this we vow."

Life as I knew it was over,
there would be no fresh start.
So I swallowed the pills
it was time to depart.
To the psych ward I went, and there I stayed
alone with myself
those were some dark days.
"Are they gone yet?" they asked, "the voices no more?"
Foolishly
I confess no.
"Then you will not walk out that door."
The medicine was crippling
I was already dead
drooling and lethargic
all I wanted was my bed.
"You're powerless," they hissed,
"better to just give in,
because remember
no matter what
we will always win."

And so it continued
precious time lost this way.
But my mother did not give up
she would fight for that day
when my eyes were finally open
clear and bright once more
when her daughter was back
and stronger than ever before.
Finally, a psychiatrist listened.
They'd give it a chance.
"We'll take you off the medicine," he said
with a hesitant glance.
So began a long process
brutal as could be
taper the drugs from my system
slowly return to being me.

When I think of it now
I was being reborn
a wiggle of toes
a thought in my head
no progress too small.
Maybe
just maybe
I was not, in fact, dead.
The voices didn't like it
not one little bit.
"We'll kill you!" they said
and I was scared
I'll admit.
"I'm not trying to hurt you
I don't need you gone.
You said you're here to stay
so can't we please get along?
I'll stop being mean to you
because, underneath it all, I know that you're hurt
and strangely enough
I think you want to protect me
no matter how covert.
You're company when I have no one
which is most of the time
and for that, I am grateful
your existence to me
it is not a crime.

So let's start fresh in our relationship
exist together as one
because I can't keep living this way
or I'll have to check out
be done."
And from that day forward
the narrative was reframed
that despite what the psychiatrists said
my voices were not the enemy

but rather derived from the pain.
Little by little, we have grown
my voices and I
through hard work and therapy
we continue to try.
They are still not very nice
always teasing and taunting
but now I know that they seek to guard me
so it is not quite as daunting.

I am okay with them now
we can co-exist
I am maybe even thankful for my voices
but don't tell them I said this.
Because without my strange friends
it took a while to see
but finally
I know
I would not be me.
I don't need the doctors to understand
a fact I now hold dear
"I am not broken," to them I say
"Let that be clear."
And if my voices were to leave me one day
I know I'd be sad
grieve their departure, their exit
feel quite a bit bad.
Because we've been through so much
navigated the stormy weather
and are still here to tell the tale
that we did it together
my voices and I.

Annie Stafford, 2020

Essential Facts about Voice Hearing

- Studies have found that between 4 and 10 percent of people across the world hear voices.

- Between 70 and 90 percent of people who hear voices do so following traumatic events.

- Voices can be male, female, without gender, child, adult, human or non-human.

- People may hear one voice or many. Some people report hearing hundreds, although, in almost all reported cases, one dominates above the others.

- Voices can be experienced in the head, in the ears, outside the head, in some other part of the body, or in the environment.

- Voices often reflect important aspects of the hearer's emotional state—emotions that are often unexpressed by the hearer.

More:
1. Voice hearing is often seen as a prime symptom of psychosis (American Psychiatric Association, 1994). Hearing voices (auditory hallucinations) is considered a first-rank

symptom of the specific psychosis of schizophrenia (Schneider, 1959). There are three main psychiatric categories of patients who hear voices: schizophrenia (around 50%); affective psychosis (around 25%); and dissociative disorders (around 80%) (Honig et al., 1998).

2. Psychiatry in our western culture unjustly identifies hearing voices with schizophrenia. Individuals who go to a psychiatrist with the experience of hearing voices have an 80% chance of getting a diagnosis of schizophrenia (Romme and Escher, 2001).

3. However, hearing voices in itself is not a symptom of an illness. Many people who hear voices find them helpful or benevolent (Romme and Escher 1993).

4. While one in three people who hear voices becomes a psychiatric patient, two in three people can cope well and are in no need of psychiatric care. No diagnosis can be given because these two out of three people who hear voices are quite healthy and function well. It is very significant that in our society, there are more people who hear voices who have never been psychiatric patients than there are people who hear voices and become psychiatric patients (Romme and Escher, 2011).

5. Brain imaging has confirmed that voice hearers do experience a sound as if there were a real person talking to them (Shergill, Brammer, Williams, Murray, and McGuire, 2000).

6. In a study of the differences between patients and non-patients who hear voices, the discrepancy was not in form but content. In other words, the non-patients heard voices both inside and outside their head, as did the patients, but either the content was positive, or the hearer had a positive view of the voice and felt in control of it. By contrast, the patients were more frightened of the voices,

the voices were more critical (malevolent), and they felt less control over them (Honig, et al., 1998).

7. Conventional psychiatric approaches to the problem of voice hearing have been to ignore the meaning of the experience for the voice hearer and concentrate on removing the symptoms (audio hallucinations) with medication (Romme and Escher, 1989). Although antipsychotic medication is helpful to some sufferers of psychosis (Fleischhaker, 2002), there is a significant portion that still experiences the "symptoms,"; that is, hearing voices despite very high doses of injected antipsychotic (Curson, Barnes, Bamber, and Weral, 1985).

8. Further, antipsychotic medication prevents the emotional processing and therefore healing of the meaning of the voices (Romme and Escher, 2000).

9. Traditional practice in behavioral psychology concentrated on either distracting the patient or ignoring references by the patient to the voice-hearing experience, with the hope that the patient would concentrate on "real" experiences, which would then be positively reinforced (the assumption being that the voice hearing was a delusional belief). The effect of this approach is to discourage the discussion about the hearing voices experience, but without eradicating it (P.D.J. Chadwick, Birchwood, and Trower, 1996).

10. In research concerning people who hear voices, it was found that in 77 percent of the people diagnosed with schizophrenia, the hearing of voices was related to traumatic experiences. These traumatic experiences varied from being sexually abused, physically abused, being extremely belittled over long periods from a young age, being neglected during long periods as a youngster, being very

aggressively treated in marriage, not being able to accept one's sexual identity, etc. (Romme and Escher, 2006).

11. Hearing voices in itself is not related to the illness of schizophrenia. In population research, only 16 percent of the whole group of voice hearers can be diagnosed with schizophrenia (Romme and Escher, 2001).

12. The prognosis of hearing voices is more positive than generally perceived. In Sandra Escher's research with children hearing voices, she followed eighty-two children over a period of four years. In that period, 64 percent of the children's voices disappeared as they learned to cope with emotions and become less stressed. For the children whose voices were pathologized and made a part of an illness, the voices did not vanish but became worse (Romme and Escher, 2006).

Montgomery County Hearing Voices Network

Key Values of the Hearing Voices Movement

- Hearing voices can be understood as a natural part of the human experience.

- Diverse explanations are accepted for the origins of the voices.

- Voice hearers are encouraged to take ownership of their experiences and define them for themselves.

- Voice hearing can be interpreted and understood in the context of life events and interpersonal narratives.

- A process of understanding and accepting one's voices may be more helpful for recovery than continual suppression and avoidance.

- Peer support and collaboration are empowering and beneficial for recovery.

Dirk Corstens, et al., Schizophrenia Bulletin Vol. 40 suppl. No. 4, pp. S285-S294, 2014

Bibliography and Suggested Reading

Anxiety and Depression

Bourne, Edmund J. *The Anxiety and Phobia Workbook*. Oakland: New Harbor Publications, Inc. 2005.

Burton, Robert. *The Anatomy of Melancholy*. New York: The New York Review of Books. First published 1621.

Casey, Nell, ed. *Unholy Ghost: Writers on Depression*. New York: HarperCollins. 2001.

Cronkite, Kathy. *On the Edge of Darkness: Conversations about Conquering Depression*. New York: Dell Publishing. 1994.

Farrington, Tim. *A Hell of Mercy: A Meditation on Depression and the Dark Night of the Soul*. New York: Harper-Collins Publishers. 2009

Ghaemi, Nassir. *A First-Rate Madness: Uncovering the Links between Leadership and Mental Illness*. New York: Penguin Books. 2011.

Manning, Martha. *Undercurrents: A Therapist's Reckoning with Her Own Depression*. New York: HarperCollins Publishers. 1994.

May, Gerald G. *The Dark Night of the Soul*. New York: HarperOne. 2004.

Merkin, Daphne. *This Close to Happy: A Reckoning with Depression*. New York: Farrar, Straus and Giroux. 2017.

Shawn, Allen. *Wish I Could Be There: Notes from a Phobic Life.* New York: Viking. 2007.

Smith, Daniel. *Monkey Mind: A Memoir of Anxiety.* New York: Simon & Schuster Paperbacks. 2012.

Solomon, Andrew. *The Noonday Demon: At Atlas of Depression.* New York: Scribner. 2001.

Stossel, Scott. *My Age of Anxiety: Fear, Hope, Dread, and the Search for Peace of Mind.* New York: Vintage Books: 2013.

Styron, William. *Darkness Visible: A Memoir of Madness.* New York: Vintage Books. 1990.

Thompson, Tracy. *The Beast: A Reckoning with Depression.* New York: G. P. Putnam's Sons. 1995.

Yapko, Michael D. *Hand-Me-Down Blues: How to Stop Depression from Spreading in Families.* New York: St. Martin's Press. 1999.

Borderline Personality Disorder

Aguirre, Blaise A. *Borderline Personality Disorder in Adolescents: A Complete Gide to Understanding and Coping When Your Adolescent has BPD.* Massachusetts: Fair Winds Press. 2007.

Friedel, Robert O. *Borderline Personality Disorder Demystified.* Cambridge: Da Capo Press. 2004.

Kreger, Randi and Mason, Paul T. *Stop Walking on Eggshells: Taking Your Life Back When Someone You Care About Has Borderline Personality Disorder.* Oakland: New Harbinger Publications, Inc. 2010.

Kreisman, Jerold J. and Straus, Hal. *I Hate You—Don't Leave Me.* New York: Avon Books. 1989.

Reiland, Rachel. *Get Me Out of Here: My Recovery from Borderline Personality Disorder.* Minnesota: Hazelden. 2004.

Van Gelder, Kiera. *The Buddha & the Borderline: My Recovery from Borderline Personality Disorder through Dialectical Behavior Therapy, Buddhism & Online Dating*. Oakland: New Harbinger Publications, Inc. 2010.

Social Anxiety Disorder

Cain, Susan. *Quiet: The Power of Introverts in a World that Can't Stop Talking*. Broadway Paperbacks. 2012.

Bakalar, Nicholas and Hollander, Eric. *Coping with Social Anxiety*. New York: Henry Holt and Company. 2005.

Barkway, Barbara and Markway, Gregory. *Painfully Shy: How to Overcome Social Anxiety and Reclaim Your Life*. New York: Thomas Dunne Books. 2001.

Chung, Michaela. *The Irresistible Introvert*. New York: Skyhorse Publishing, Inc. 2016.

Lane, Christopher. *Shyness: How Normal Behavior Became a Sickness*. New Haven & London: Yale University Press. 2007.

Laney, Marti Olsen. *The Introvert Advantage: How to Thrive in an Extrovert World*. New York: Workman Publishing Company, Inc. 2002.

Zimbardo, Philip. *Shyness: What It Is, What to Do About It*. New York: Perseus Books Group 1977.

Bipolar Disorder

Cheney, Terri. *Manic: A Memoir*. New York: Harper. 2008.

Fanning, Arnold Thomas. *Mind on Fire: A Memoir of Madness and Recovery*. UK: Penguin Random House UK. 2018.

Green, Rosalie. *Bipolar Kids: Helping Your Child Find Calm in the Mood Storm*. Philadelphia: Da Capo Press. 2007.

Jamison, Kay Redfield. *Touched with Fire: Manic-Depressive Illness and the Artistic Temperament.* New York: Free Press Paperbacks. 1993.

Jamison, Kay Redfield. *An Unquiet Mind.* New York: Alfred A. Knopf. 1995.

McManamy, John. *Living Well with Depression and Bipolar Disorder.* New York: HarperCollins. 2006.

Miklowitz, David and George, Elizabeth. *The Bipolar Teen: What You Can Do to Help Your Family.* New York: The Guilford Press. 2008.

Raeburn, Paul. *Acquainted with the Night: A Parent's Quest to Understand Depression and Bipolar Disorder in His Children.* New York: Broadway Books. 2004.

Steel, Danielle. *His Bright Light: The Story of Nick Traina.* New York: Dell Publishing. 1998.

Obsessive-Compulsive Disorder

Frankl, Viktor E. *The Unheard Cry for Meaning: Psychotherapy and Humanism.* New York: Simon and Schuster. 1978.

Laverton, Steven. *Obsessive-Compulsive Disorders: Treating and Understanding Crippling Habits.* New York: Warner Books, Inc. 1991.

Maloney, Beth Alison. *Saving Sammy: Curing the Boy Who Caught OCD.* New York: Crown Publishers. 2009.

Osborn, Ian. *Tormenting Thoughts & Secret Rituals: The Hidden Epidemic of Obsessive-Compulsive Disorder.* New York: Pantheon Books. 1998.

Patterson, James and Friedman, Hal. *Med Head: My Knock-Down, Drag-Out, Drugged-up Battle with my Brain.* New York: Little, Brown and Company. 2009.

Rapoport, Judith. *The Boy Who Couldn't Stop Washing: The Experience and Treatment of Obsessive-Compulsive Disorder.* New York: Penguin Books. 1989.

Traig, Jennifer. *Devil in the Details: Scenes from an Obsessive Girlhood.* New York: Little, Brown and Company: 2004.

Psychotic Disorders

Granata, Vince. *Everything is Fine.* New York: Atria Books. 2021.

Greenberg, Joanne. *I Never Promised You a Rose Garden.* New York: Signet. 1964.

Greenberg, Michael. *Hurry Down Sunshine: A Father's Story of Love and Madness.* New York: Vintage Books. 2008.

Hall, Will. *Outside Mental Health: Voices and Visions of Madness.* New York: Madness Radio. 2016.

Karon, Bertram and Vandenbos, Gary. *Psychotherapy of Schizophrenia.* Northvale: Jason Aronson, Inc. 1981.

Kolker, Robert. *Hidden Valley Road: Inside the Mind of an American Family.* New York: Doubleday. 2020.

Powers, Ron. *No One Cares About Crazy People: The Chaos and Heartbreak of Mental Health in America.* New York: Hachette Brook Group. 2017.

Saks, Elyn R. *The Center Cannot Hold: My Journey through Madness.* New York: Hyperion. 2007.

"I'm Elyn Saks and This is What it's like to Live with Schizophrenia." Dvorsky, George. https://io9.gizmodo.com/5983970/im-elyn-saks-and-this-is-what-its-like-to-live-with-schizophrenia, Wikipedia, https://en.wikipedia.org/wiki/Psychosis, (17 November 2017). April 2, 2018.

Sechehaye, Marguerite. *Autobiography of a Schizophrenic Girl.* New York: Grune & Stratton, Inc. 1951.

Tracey, Patrick. *Stalking Irish Madness: Searching for the Roots of My Family's Schizophrenia*. New York: Bantam Books. 2008.

Wagner, Pamela Spiro and Spiro, Carolyn S., M.D. *Divided Minds: Twin Sisters and Their Journey Through Schizophrenia*. New York: St. Martin's Press. 2005.

Weijun Wang, Esme. *The Collected Schizophrenias*. Minneapolis: Graywolf Press. 2019.

Williams, Paris. *Rethinking Madness: Towards a Paradigm Shift in Our Understanding and Treatment of Psychosis*. San Rafael: Sky's Edge Publishing. 2012.

Suicide

Alvarez, A. *The Savage God: A Study of Suicide*. New York: W.W. Norton & Company. 1990

Antrim, Donald. *One Friday in April*. New York: W. W. Norton & Company. 2021.

Bialosky, Jill. *History of a Suicide: My Sister's Unfinished Life*. New York: Atria Books. 2011.

Griffith, Gail. *Will's Choice: A Suicidal Teen, a Desperate Mother, and a Chronicle of Recovery*. New York: Harper. 2006.

Jamison, Kay Redfield. *Night Falls Fast: Understanding Suicide*. New York: Vintage Books. 1999.

Klebold, Sue. *A Mother's Reckoning: Living in the Aftermath of Tragedy*. New York: Penguin Random House. 2016.

Quinnett, Paul G. *Counseling Suicidal People: A Therapy of Hope*. QPR Institute. 2009.

Raskin, Jamie. *Unthinkable: Trauma, Truth, and the Trials of American Democracy*. New York: HarperCollins. 2022.

Solomon, Andrew. *The Mystifying Rise of Child Suicide: A Family Tragedy Sheds Light on a Burgeoning Mental-Health Emergency.* The New Yorker: April 11, 2022.

Trauma

Allen, Jon G. *Coping with Trauma: A Guide to Self-Understanding.* Washington, DC: American Psychiatric Press, Inc. 1995.

Harris, Nadine Burke. *The Deepest Well: Healing the Long-Term Effects of Childhood Adversity.* New York: Houghton Mifflin Harcourt. 2018.

Levine, Peter. *Waking the Tiger: Healing Trauma.* California: North Atlantic Books. 1997.

Terr, Lenore. *Too Scared to Cry: Psychic Trauma in Childhood.* New York: Basic Books. 1990.

Van der Kolk, Bessel. *The Body Keeps the Score: Brain, Mind, and Body in the Healing of Trauma.* New York: Penguin Books. 2014.

Hearing Voices

Baker, Paul. *The Voice Inside: A Practical Guide for and About People Who Hear Voices.* Port of Ness, Isle of Lewis: P & P Press. 2009.

Bennett, Amanda and Schiller, Lori. *The Quiet Room: A Journey out of the Torment of Madness.* New York: Grand Central Publishing. 1994.

Callahan, Sidney. *Women Who Hear Voices: The Challenge of Religious Experience.* New York: Paulist Press. 2003.

Coleman, Ron and Longden, Eleanor. *Recovery: An Alien Concept?* Port of Ness, Island of Lewis: P & P Press, 2011.

Corstens, Dirk, Dillon, Jacqui, Escher, Sandra; Morris, Mervyn and Romme, Marius. *Living with Voices: 50 Stories of Recovery.* UK: PCCS Books, Ltd. 2009.

Dent Pearce, Louisa. *The Little Girl that Nobody Wanted.* Melbourne: Elleldi Studios. 2011.

Dorman, Daniel. *Dante's Cure: A Journey out of Madness.* New York: Other Press LLC. 2003.

Fernyhough, Charles. *The Voices Within: The History and Science of How we Talk to Ourselves.* New York: Basic Books. 2016.

Gutkovich, Dmitriy. *Life with Voices: A Guide for Harmony.* 2020.

Hornstein, Gail. *Agnes's Jacket: A Psychologist's Search for the Meaning of Madness.* New York: Rodale. 2009.

Longden, Eleanor. *Learning from the Voices in my Head.* TED talk. 2013.

McCarthy-Jones, Simon. *Can't You Hear Them? The Science and Significance of Hearing Voices.* London and Philadelphia: Jessica Kingsley Publishers. 2017.

North, Carol. *Welcome, Silence: My Triumph Over Schizophrenia.* New York: Simon & Schuster. 1987.

Runningwolf, Michael. *The Promise.* Amazon Books: 2019.

Smith, Daniel B. *Muses, Madmen and Prophets: Hearing Voices and the Borders of Sanity.* New York: Penguin Books. 2007.

Steele, Ken and Berman, Claire. *The Day the Voices Stopped: A Memoir of Madness and Hope.* New York: Basic Books. 2001.

"The Sound of Madness: Can We Treat Psychosis by Listening to the Voices in our Heads?" *Harper's Magazine.* May 2018. T. M. Luhrmann. https://harpers.org/archive/2018/06/the-sound-of-madness/.5/22/2018.

"The Voices in our Heads: Why Do People Talk to Themselves, and When Does it Become a Problem?" *The New Yorker.* January 9, 2017. Jerome Groopman. https://www.newyorker.com/magazine/2017/01/09/the-voices-in-our-heads. 12/4/2017.

Woods, Angela. *"The Art of Medicine: Voices, Identity, and Meaning-Making."* The Lancet, Vol. 386. December 12, 2015. www.thelancet.com. December 20, 2017.

Associated Reading

Aguirre, Blaise A., Kaplan, Cynthia S. and Rater, Michael. *Helping Your Troubled Teen.* Massachusetts: Fair Winds Press. 2007.

Cherry, Charles L. *A Quiet Haven: Quakers, Moral Treatment, and Asylum Reform.* Cranbury: Associated University Presses. 1989.

Cohen-Sandler, Roni and Silver, Michelle. *I'm Not Mad, I Just Hate You! A New Understanding of Mother-Daughter Conflict.* New York: Penguin Books. 1999.

Corbett, Lionel. *The Religious Function of the Psyche.* New York: Routledge. 1996.

Dickens, Charles. *Bleak House.* New York: Penguin Putnam Inc. 1853.

Dudman, Martha Tod. *Augusta, Gone.* New York: Simon & Schuster. 2001.

Epstein, Mark, MD. *The Zen of Therapy: Uncovering a Hidden Kindness in Life.* New York: Penguin Press. 2022.

Faber, Adele, Mazlish, Elaine. *How to Talk so Teens Will Listen & Listen so Teens Will Talk.* HarperCollins, Publishers: New York. 2005.

Fox, Matthew. *Original Blessing: A Primer in Creation Spirituality.* New York: Jeremy P. Tarcher/Putnam. 2000.

Gottlieb, Daniel. *Voices in the Family: A Therapist Talks about Listening, Openness & Healing.* New York: Sterling Publishing Co., Inc. 2007.

Gottlieb, Lori. *Maybe You Should Talk to Someone. A Therapist, Her Therapist, and Our Lives Revealed.* New York: Houghton Mifflin Harcourt Publishing Company. 2019.

Grof, S., & Grof, D. *Spiritual Emergency: When Personal Transformation Becomes a Crisis.* New York: St. Martin's Press. 1989.

Grof, S. & Grof, D. *Understanding and Treatment of Psychospiritual Crises.* International Journal of Transpersonal Studies. Volume 36, Issue 2, Article 5. September 1, 2017. https:// digitalcommons.ciis.edu/ijts-transpersonalstudies/vol36/iss2/5/ .July 226, 2018.

Gutkind, Lee, ed. *Show Me All Your Scars: True Stories of Living with Mental Illness.* Pittsburgh: In Fact Books. 2016.

"History of Mental Health Treatment, 1800s – 2000s." https://www.dualdiagnosis.org/mental-health-and-addiction/ history/.May 31, 2018.

Hornstein, Gail A. *To Redeem One Person is to Redeem the World: The Life of Frieda Fromm-Reichmann.* New York: Other Press. 2000.

Hunt, Marcia, Resnick, Sandra. *"Two Birds, One Stone: Unintended Consequences and a Potential Solution for Problems with Recovery in Mental Health."* Psychiatric Services 66:11. November 2015.

Inman, Susan. *After Her Brain Broke: Helping My Daughter Recover Her Sanity.* Ontario: Bridgeross Communications. 2010.

Insel, Thomas. *Healing: Our Path from Mental Illness to Mental Health.* New York: Penguin Press. 2022.

James, William. *The Varieties of Religious Experience: A Study in Human Nature.* New York: Macmillan, 1961.

James, William. *The Will to Believe and Other Essays in Popular Philosophy.* New York: Dover Publications, Inc. 1956.

Kearney, Michael. *Mortally Wounded: Stories of Soul Pain, Death, and Healing.* New York: Scribner. 1996.

Kennedy, Patrick & Fried, Stephen. *A Common Struggle: A Personal*

Journey through the Past and Future of Mental Illness and Addiction. New York: Blue Rider Press. 2015.

Mackler, Daniel and Morrissey, Matthew. *A Way Out of Madness: Dealing with Your Family After You've Been Diagnosed with a Psychiatric Disorder*. Bloomington: AuthorHouse. 2010.

McGraw, Patricia Romano. *It's Not Your Fault: How Healing Relationships Change Your Brain & Can Help You Overcome a Painful Past*. Wilmette: Bahai Publishing. 2004.

Mehl-Madrona, Lewis. *Healing the Mind through the Power of Story: The Promise of Narrative Psychiatry*. Vermont: Bear & Company. 2010.

Miller, Alice. *The Drama of the Gifted Child: The Search for the True Self*. New York: Basic Books, Inc. 1981.

Moore, Thomas. *The Soul's Religion: Cultivating a Profoundly Spiritual Way of Life*. New York: HarperCollins. 2002.

Mosher, Loren R. and Hendrix, Voyce. *Soteria: Through Madness to Deliverance*. Xlibris Corporation. 2004.

Palmer, Parker. *Let Your Life Speak: Listening for the Voice of Vocation*. John Wiley & Sons, Inc. 2000.

Pipher, Mary. *The Shelter of Each Other: Rebuilding our Families*. New York: G. P. Putnam's Sons. 1996.

Pipher, Mary. *Reviving Ophelia: Saving the Selves of Adolescent Girls*. New York: The Random House Publishing Group. 1994.

Plath, Sylvia. *The Bell Jar*. New York: Harper & Row. 1971.

Poncho, Dennis. *Because I Love You: The Program*. Dennis Poncher and Patricia Schwartz: 1986.

Powell, John, J.S. *Why Am I Afraid to Tell You Who I Am?* Texas: RCL Benziger. 1969.

"Psychosis as a Spiritual Crisis: An Opportunity for Growth,"

Michael Cornwall, Ph. D.
https://www.madinamerica.com/2012/ 09/psychosis-as-a-
spiritual-crisis-an-opportunity-for-growth. July 24, 2018.

"The Retreat, York, England." Quakers in the World.
www.quakersintheworld.org/quakers-in-action/92/The-Retreat-
York-England. March 30, 201.

"Shamanic Extraction." https://www.shamanlinks.net/shaman-
info/shamanic-healing/shamanic-extraction/. July 23, 2018.

Sheff, David. *Beautiful Boy: A Father's Journey Through His Son's
Addiction.* Boston: Houghton Mifflin Company. 2008.

Shorto, Russell. *Saints and Madmen: Psychiatry Opens its Doors to
Religion.* New York: Henry Holt and Company, LLC. 1999.

Simmons, Rachel. *Odd Girl Out: The Hidden Culture of Aggression
in Girls.* Orlando: Harcourt, Inc. 2002.

Sogyal Rinpoche. *The Tibetan Book of Living and Dying.* New York:
HarperCollins Publishers. 2002.ch

Stein, Murray. *In Midlife: A Jungian Perspective.* Connecticut: Spring
Publications, Inc. 1983.

Stepp, Laura Sessions. *Our Last Best Shot: Guiding our Children
through Early Adolescence.* New York: Penguin Putnam, Inc.
2000.

Whitaker, Robert. *Anatomy of an Epidemic.* New York: Broadway
Paperbacks. 2010.

Winfrey, Oprah & Perry, Bruce D. *What Happened to You?
Conversations on Trauma, Resilience and Healing.* New York:
Flatiron Books. 2021.

Young-Eisendrath, Polly. *The Resilient Spirit: Transforming
Suffering into Insight and Renewal.* Massachusetts: Da Capo
Press. 1996.

About Atmosphere Press

Atmosphere Press is an independent, full-service publisher for excellent books in all genres and for all audiences. Learn more about what we do at atmospherepress.com.

We encourage you to check out some of Atmosphere's latest releases, which are available at Amazon.com and via order from your local bookstore:

The Great Unfixables, by Neil Taylor

Soused at the Manor House, by Brian Crawford

Portal or Hole: Meditations on Art, Religion, Race And The Pandemic, by Pamela M. Connell

A Walk Through the Wilderness, by Dan Conger

The House at 104: Memoir of a Childhood, by Anne Hegnauer

A Short History of Newton Hall, Chester, by Chris Fozzard

Serial Love: When Happily Ever After... Isn't, by Kathy Kay

Sit-Ins, Drive-Ins and Uncle Sam, by Bill Slawter

Black Water and Tulips, by Sara Mansfield Taber

Ghosted: Dating & Other Paramoural Experiences, by Jana Eisenstein

Walking with Fay: My Mother's Uncharted Path into Dementia, by Carolyn Testa

FLAWED HOUSES of FOUR SEASONS, by James Morris

Word for New Weddings, by David Glusker and Thom Blackstone

It's Really All about Collaboration and Creativity! A Textbook and Self-Study Guide for the Instrumental Music Ensemble Conductor, by John F. Colson

A Life of Obstructions, by Rob Penfield

Troubled Skies Over Quaker Hill: A Search for the Truth, by Lessie Auletti

About the Author

Tricia Stafford was born and raised in Brooklyn, NY, and currently resides in Montgomery County, PA. She has an MA in English Literature from the City University of NY and an MA in Liberal Studies from Villanova University in PA. She is the Executive Director of Tend to Hope, a nonprofit organization she created with her daughter Annie to inspire hope in individuals in mental health crisis facilities.